THE WATTS HISTORY OF SPORTS

the final four

FRANKLIN WATTS
A Division of Scholastic Inc.
New York • Toronto • London • Auckland • Sydney
Mexico City • New Delhi • Hong Kong
Danbury, Connecticut

MARK STEWART

Researched and Edited by
MIKE KENNEDY

Cover design by Dave Klaboe   Series design by Molly Heron

Cover photo IDs: (center left) UCLA coach John Wooden after the team's victory in the 1971 Final Four; (center right) Indiana State forward/center Larry Bird during March 1979 Final Four; (clockwise from upper left) University of Connecticut guard Rickey Moore cuts down the net at the Division 1 Championship, Tropicana Field, March 1999; University of Arizona head coach Lute Olson at the Final Four in April 2001; Cover of Sports Illustrated 1974; Duke's Shane Battier in the NCAA Championship against Arizona in April 2001; Tipoff with Duke forward Elton Brand (41) and University of Connecticut center Jake Voskuhl (43) at Tropicana Field, March 1999; Cover of a special basketball issue of Sports Review from 1961; Jerry Lucas (11) of Ohio State in action against St. Joseph's in 1961.

Photographs © 2002: AllSport USA/Getty Images: 97 (Jonathan Daniel); AP/Wide World Photos: 117 (Jeffrey Camarati), 119 (Rich Clarkson/NCAA Photo), cover bottom right, cover left center, 71, 83; Corbis Images: 4 (Bettmann), 6 (Dick McEvilly/Bettmann), 23 (Herbie Scharfman/Bettmann); Icon Sports Media/John McDonough: 1; NCAA Photos/Rich Clarkson and Associates: 7 (AP/Wide World Photos), cover center left, cover center right, 27, 31, 38, 40, 43, 44, 45, 46, 48, 51, 52, 56, 58, 60, 61, 63, 64, 65, 67, 74, 75, 77, 79, 81, 85, 86, 88, 90, 93, 99, 101, 104, 106, 115 (Rich Clarkson), 108 (Brian Gadbery), cover top left, cover bottom center, 112 (David Gonzales), cover top center (Ryan McKee), 17 (Seattle Times), 13 (University of Wyoming), 11, 21, 36; Sporting News: 35, 41; Team Stewart, Inc.: cover bottom left, cover top right, 10, 12, 16, 18, 20, 22, 24, 28, 29, 32, 33, 49, 68, 69, 95, 102.

Library of Congress Cataloging-in-Publication Data

Stewart, Mark
    The Final Four / Mark Stewart.
    p. cm. — (The Watts history of sports)
    Includes index.
    Summary: Discusses the championship round of the NCAA basketball
    tournaments, including powerhouse teams, exciting games, and
    outstanding players from past years.
    ISBN 0-531-11951-3 (lib. bdg.)
    1. NCAA Basketball Tournament—History—Juvenile literature.
    [1. NCAA Basketball Tournament—History.
    2. Basketball—Tournaments—History.] I. Title. II. Series.
    796.323'63'0973—dc21   2001007183
                                                        CIP

CONTENTS

New York sportswriter Ned Irish, the first to recognize the moneymaking potential of college basketball. America may have been in the depths of the Great Depression, but sports fans were willing to spend what little they had, to see the nation's best schools compete in tournament play.

INTRODUCTION

The idea of a national college basketball tournament sprang from the fertile mind of a man named Ned Irish. A sports reporter for the *New York World Telegram* in the 1930s, Irish was often assigned to cover the city's many college basketball games. These contests were held in tiny gymnasiums, and as the sport gained in popularity during the 1920s and 1930s, it was not unusual to see several hundred people turned away, even on a weeknight. Irish, who claimed he once had to crawl through a gym window just to report on one game, noticed that these spectators were not just bored college students looking for something to do on a winter evening. There were many adult fans following the sport. Irish reasoned that if four of these teams were to meet in, say, Madison Square Garden, thousands would come to see them.

In January 1931, Irish helped *World Telegram* sports editor Dan Daniel stage a triple-header featuring the great St. John's University team. The event was held to raise money for mayor Jimmy Walker's Unemployment Relief Fund. It was a wintry night during the depths of the Great Depression, yet more than 15,000 spectators paid to view three great basketball games. Convinced that his concept would work, Irish began planning his first major event. It finally happened in December 1934. Again, more than 15,000 people walked through the turnstiles. The doubleheader featured two New York schools—St. John's and New York University—and two "imports"—popular Notre Dame and Westminster, a school from Pennsylvania with one of the nation's top players.

By the end of the 1934–35 season, Irish had booked eight more basketball events, and each was a success. In all, 99,528 fans bought tickets to watch the college stars play.

The formula of mixing popular local teams with out-of-town squads was a smart one. Basketball was still evolving, and schools played very differently depending on where they were from. Fans loved seeing things they had never seen before. After each event, coaches would take what they learned from opponents, work it into their games, and introduce it to the other schools in their conferences. In December 1935, Irish invited Stanford University to one of his events. The Indians were predicted to be chewed up and spit out by Long Island University, which was riding a 43-game winning streak.

Stanford broke the streak, however thanks to a sophomore named Hank Luisetti. In an era where everyone shot the ball with two hands, Luisetti shot with one, and he could do so while jumping or on the run. The LIU players had no idea how to stop him, and he led Stanford to a 45-31 victory. Soon every player in New York was practicing the "running one-hander."

By 1938, it was time for Irish to take the next big step. He put together a group of investors and created the National Invitation Tournament (NIT). Because the National Collegiate Athletic Association (NCAA) had no year-end competition, the NIT became the unofficial championship of college basketball. Held in Madison Square Garden, the nation's most famous sports arena, the NIT became an instant success. During the 1940s, more than 500,000 people attended these round-robin tournaments.

The NCAA, also looking to take advantage of basketball's popularity, started its own tournament. In 1939, with the blessing of the NCAA, the National Association of Basketball Coaches (NABC) held the first

event. Although the NIT got more publicity and attracted better schools—and would continue doing so for a decade—the first NCAA Tournament was a success. Run on a shoestring budget by a bunch of coaches and their assistants, it did well enough to convince the NCAA not only to continue the event, but also to take the tournment off the NABC's hands.

The modern era of college basketball had begun.

Louisville and Western Kentucky square off in National Invitation Tournament action. For many years the NIT was more popular than the NCAA Tournament.

CHAPTER 1

1939–1949

1939
Oregon Ducks
Oklahoma Sooners
Ohio State Buckeyes
Villanova Wildcats

In the 1930s, the formula for winning basketball tournaments was a bit different than it is today. Students were not used to traveling great distances and visiting new cities. The boredom of long train trips and the excitement of new places often sapped the players' energy on the court. That is why Howard Hobson, coach of the Oregon Ducks, decided to accept an invitation to one of Ned Irish's early-season tournaments at New York's Madison Square Garden. On the trip, Oregon played games in Iowa, Illinois, Michigan, Ohio, and Pennsylvania. Hobson was already thinking about the NCAA's new, year-end competition to decide the champion of college basketball.

He knew he had a good team; nicknamed the "Tall Firs" after the towering forests of the Pacific Northwest, the Oregon players were indeed giants in their day. The Ducks' All-American center, "Slim" Wintermute, stood 6-foot-8. Like most big men of his era, he was a slow, lumbering fellow. His main job was to shove opposing

centers away from the backboard, and also to hit a few close-range shots during the game. What made Wintermute more effective than other centers were the two players with whom he shared the Oregon front line.

Ohio State's John Schick rises to the rim against Oregon. Oregon's "Tall Firs" prevailed in the first NCAA championship game.

Laddie Gale was the top scorer in the Pacific Coast Conference, while John Dick played an excellent all-around game. Both forwards stood just a shade under 6-foot-5 and were excellent rebounders. The team's top "sapling" was Bobby Anet, an ambitious floor general who knew how to get the ball into the hands of his scorers.

Eight universities—Oregon, Texas, Oklahoma, Utah State, Villanova, Brown, Wake Forest, and Ohio State—accepted invitations to the first NCAA Tournament. Regional Semifinals were held in Philadelphia and San Francisco. Thus, what fans think of as the first Final Four was actually a pair of Final Twos. The tournament's second round was also played in Philadelphia and San Francisco. Not until the early 1950s would all four schools meet in the same building for the final games.

Of the four schools that reached this point in 1939, only Oregon had done any extensive traveling. That is not to say they would have it easy. The Ducks' first opponent, Oklahoma, had two formidable stars in Herb Scheffler and Marvin Mesch. Hobson instructed Anet to feed the ball to his three big men, who had a size advantage over the Sooners. Unable to stop the Tall Firs, Scheffler and Mesch immediately found themselves in foul trouble. Oregon grabbed an early lead and held it the whole way to win 55-37.

Back east, Ohio State squared off against Villanova to decide who would face Oregon in the first NCAA Final. The Buckeyes had the tournament's most potent scorer in Jimmy Hull. He hit for 28 against the Wildcats, while Villanova's top shooter, Paul Nugent, could muster only 16. Ohio State triumphed, 53-36.

The Ducks and the Buckeyes met for the championship, which was held on the campus of Northwestern University in Evanston, Illinois. Although this venue was much closer to home for the Ohioans than for the Oregonians, Coach Hobson's players seemed far less drained by the travel than their opponents. Ohio State performed sluggishly in the first half, as Oregon played a tight, harassing defense and ran the fast break whenever possible. In the locker room with a 21-16 halftime lead, the Ducks decided to pick up the pace even more in the second period. The fatigued Buckeyes strained to keep up, but in the end they could not. The 46-33 win was so easy that Anet never bothered to call a time-out; he did not see any point in allowing his opponents to catch their breath. The Ducks relished their trip back to campus. Once their train entered Oregon, it stopped at almost every station along the way so that the townspeople could honor and cheer their champions.

Champion: Oregon
Winning Coach: Howard Hobson
Number of Schools in Tournament: 8
Best Player: Jimmy Hull, Ohio State

1940
Duquesne Dukes
Indiana Hoosiers
Kansas Jayhawks
Southern California Trojans

Basketball in the early 1940s was still evolving. Many fans do not realize that until 1938, play was stopped after each basket and a jump ball was held at center court. A team with an earthbound center could actually go several minutes without touching the ball! Once this rule was changed and the defensive team automatically gained possession after a basket, coaching strategies differed on what to do next. Some coaches, such as Forrest "Phog" Allen of Kansas (who learned the game from basketball's inventor, Dr. James Naismith), still saw basketball as a kind of indoor football. The ball was advanced slowly, and set plays were called. After a swirl of X's and O's that could last a minute or more (there was no shot clock back then), an open man might get a good look at the basket and attempt a shot. If not, another play would be called, and the faking and cutting and passing would start all over again. To combat this strategy, coaches also devised complex defensive schemes. A smart, disciplined defense could stop just about any kind of play. Indeed, when two good defensive squads played, they sometimes scored fewer than 20 baskets—combined!

Other coaches, like 31-year-old Branch McCracken of the Indiana Hoosiers, believed basketball was a game that was best played at top speed. He favored pushing the ball up the court before an opponent's defense could set itself. Like other coaches, he diagrammed set plays for his offense, but McCracken also urged his players to be creative and grab opportunities whenever they presented themselves. His team was nicknamed the "Hurryin' Hoosiers." Although others had tinkered with fast-break basketball, it was McCracken who proved you could win championships with it. Each man on the Hoosiers could run the floor and hit a driving layup, which often was enough to send enemy defenders into a panic.

This was McCracken's strategy against Duquesne in the eastern half of the Final Four. Center Bill Menke scored 10 points for the Hoosiers, while Curly Armstrong and Harry Schaefer combined for 15. Chick Davies, who coached the Dukes, knew his players were as good or better than McCracken's, but he never figured out a way to stop them. When his two stars, Moe Becker and Mel Milkovich, fouled out in the second half, Davies did not know what to do. He watched helplessly as Indiana rolled to a 39-30 victory.

Out west, Kansas upset the Trojans 43-42. The Jayhawks managed to control USC's Ralph Vaughn, the nation's best player, but Dick Sears broke loose for 19 points and helped his team build a 6-point lead late in the second half. Kansas, led by Dick Harp, cut USC's lead to 42-41 with under a minute left. With the Trojans hoping to run out the clock, Kansas's Bob Allen (the coach's son) stole a pass and fed teammate Bob Engleman. His shot from the corner went in with 16 seconds left, and the Jayhawks hung on for a heart-stopping 43-42 win.

By now most fans expected Kansas to win the final. After the NCAA took over the tournament, officials had asked Coach Allen to help make it a moneymaker. He agreed to get involved, and one of his first acts was to relocate the final to Kansas City, an hour or so from his campus in Lawrence, Kansas. With the crowd on the Jayhawks' side, the invading Hoosiers definitely had their work cut out for them.

The game began as everyone expected. Allen's team controlled the ball for long stretches, and Indiana struggled to get its running game going. In fact, the Hoosiers did not score their first basket until midway through the first half. At that point, however, McCracken's players began to

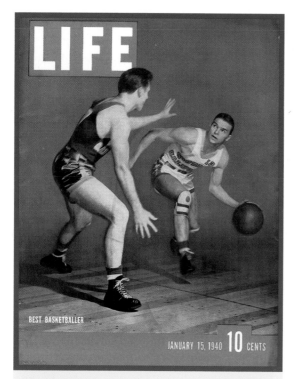

USC's Ralph Vaughn eyes the basket in a posed shot for the cover of *Life* magazine. Vaughn was the first basketball star to make the cover of *Life*.

turn the tide. They forced Kansas to take poor shots and beat the Jayhawks down the floor for some easy baskets. Led by Marv Huffman and Jay McCreary, the Hoosiers were up 32-19 at halftime. Facing a huge deficit, Allen now had to make a decision. It would be almost impossible to make back that much lost ground with his slow-moving offense. Would he be willing to pick up the pace and do a little running? Never! Allen continued to grind out points the old-fashioned way, and Kansas fell further behind. The stubborn coach watched as his team went down in flames, 60-42.

> **Champion: Indiana**
> **Winning Coach: Branch McCracken**
> **Number of Schools in Tournament: 8**
> **Best Player: Marv Huffman, Indiana**

1941

Arkansas Razorbacks
Pittsburgh Panthers
Washington State Cougars
Wisconsin Badgers

When you finish ninth in the Big Ten Conference, you cannot go much lower. That is where the Wisconsin Badgers ended up in 1939–40. When their 1940–41 season opened with a humiliating loss to Minnesota, some fans worried that they might actually finish tenth this time. Coach Bud Foster was not worried. In his mind, the Badgers were a tough, talented team that was the equal of any in the country. He was right. By season's end, they were conference champs and the proud owners of a 12-game winning streak. Center Gene Englund and forward Johnny Kotz led the Badgers into the NCAA Tournament, where they edged Dartmouth by a single point to make the Final Four.

The favorite to take the championship was Washington State, which was led by big Paul Lindemann. Arkansas, with high-scoring Johnny Adams, was also a dangerous team. These two schools would meet in the western final, while Wisconsin was scheduled to play Pittsburgh, one of only three teams to beat the Badgers during the season.

In the Arkansas-Washington State game, Razorbacks coach Glen Rose knew his team had to hold Lindemann in check.

The 6-foot-7 center had burned Creighton for 26 points in the opening round. Jack Friel, the coach of the Cougars, was equally worried about Adams, whose ability to shoot while in the air made him hard to defend. Arkansas did a decent job on Lindemann, but Washington State was more than a one-man show. Vern Butts scored 11 points and Kirk Gebert hit for 12 as the Cougars stunned the Razorbacks with a great first-half shooting display. Despite the second-half heroics of Adams, Arkansas never got close, and the game ended 64-53.

The eastern final was played on Wisconsin's home floor, but that did not seem to bother Doc Carlson's Panthers. Pittsburgh defended well against the Badgers and got a big first half from Ed Straloski. The second half, however, belonged to Englund and the Badgers. The big man created all sorts of problems inside for the Panthers, and Wisconsin managed to churn out a workman-like 36-30 victory.

Coach Foster faced a dilemma in the championship game. He knew his boys could handle Lindemann, but he feared the other Cougars would start hitting shots, just as they had against Arkansas. Assistant Fritz Wagner convinced his boss that Butts and Gebert would not be able to repeat their performances. Foster double-teamed Lindemann all game and dared Washington State to shoot from outside. Try as they might, the Cougars simply could not make their shots. During a 9-minute stretch in the first half, they failed to score a single point. Wisconsin took a slim lead into the second half and held it to the end, when the Badgers scored five unanswered points to put the game away, 39-34. The laughingstock of the Big Ten in 1940 had the last laugh in 1941.

Bud Foster's Wisconsin Badgers, the 1941 NCAA champions.

Champion: Wisconsin
Winning Coach: Bud Foster
Number of Schools in Tournament: 8
Best Player: Johnny Kotz,
Wisconsin

1942
Colorado Buffaloes
Dartmouth Indians
Kentucky Wildcats
Stanford Indians

Everyone was picking Colorado or Kentucky when the 1942 NCAA Tournament was whittled down to four teams. Both schools had good, disciplined players and were coached by disciples of the legendary Phog Allen. Colorado's Frosty Cox not only served as an assistant to Allen in Kansas, but also recruited much of his team in the state—right out from under the old man's nose. Adolph Rupp of Kentucky also learned the game under Allen. His Wildcats made headlines after upsetting Illinois in the first round.

Despite expectations of a Colorado-Kentucky final, the two other teams that had made it this far were not to be taken lightly. Dartmouth's James Olsen and George Munroe had nearly propelled the Indians to the Final Four a year earlier. They knew what it took to win in tournament play. Stanford, meanwhile, had Jim Pollard, one of the best players in the country.

The Wildcats lived up to their name in the opening minutes of their game against Dartmouth. They went wild at both ends of the floor and grabbed a quick lead. The Indians defense tightened up after that, and the Kentucky offense began to falter. For the rest

of the game they performed without their usual confidence and shot horrendously. Rupp watched in agony from the sideline as his dreams of a championship went up in smoke. Incredibly, Dartmouth held Kentucky to just ten baskets in a 48-28 blowout.

In another surprising result, Stanford polished off Colorado with a clever defensive effort. Every time the Buffaloes brought the ball across midcourt, they saw a different zone or man-to-man coverage. For much of the contest, they looked totally lost. Pollard scored 17 points for Stanford in an easy 46-35 win.

The two coaches in the final knew each other well. Dartmouth's Ozzie Cowles and

As this early basketball card shows, do-it-all Howie Dallmar parlayed his college stardom into a pro career. While playing for the Philadelphia Warriors, he also coached at the University of Pennsylvania.

Stanford's Everett Dean had both played for Carleton College in the 1920s, and they were good friends. Dartmouth became the favorite when it was learned that Pollard had come down with a sinus infection. Dartmouth was also without a key player, however. Team leader Bob Meyers had suffered an ankle injury in the Kentucky game and would not be at full strength.

The first half went back and forth, with neither school able to carve out much of a lead. In the second half, Dartmouth looked to be on the verge of a breakthrough when Howie Dallmar took over for Stanford. The big forward filled Pollard's role by sweeping the boards clean and igniting the Stanford fast break. Jack Dana and Ed Voss also contributed important baskets in Pollard's absence. A late run by Stanford turned a close contest into a laugher, as Stanford took the title, 53-38.

Wiry Kenny Sailors (at right of trophy) poses with his fellow Cowboys after the 1943 championship game.

Champion: Stanford
Winning Coach: Everett Dean
Number of Schools in Tournament: 8
Best Player: Howie Dallmar, Stanford

1943
DePaul Blue Demons
Georgetown Hoyas
Texas Longhorns
Wyoming Cowboys

A cloud hung over the 1943 NCAA Tournament. The United States had been involved in World War II (1939–45) for more than a year, and things were not going well. An enormous number of college students had decided to enlist after the school year ended. This group included many of the players who would be vying for the national championship. No one wanted to say it, but fans knew that some of the young men they were watching would not be alive when the 1944 tournament rolled around. Wyoming's Ken Sailors was one of the many competitors in the tournament who planned to join the fighting. He had already arranged to become an officer in the Marine Corps, one of the more dangerous jobs in the war. After the tournament there would be final exams, and then the junior would be off to Virginia for training.

Sailors was one of the country's most talked-about players. A terrific ball handler, he would put a few feet between himself and a defender, then pop straight in the air and, at the top of his jump, shoot the ball with one hand while steadying it with the other. Today's fans recognize this as a jump shot, perhaps the most common of all offensive plays, but fans in the 1940s believed it to be a fad. The methods most used for shooting a basketball back then were the hook shot, the standing set shot (both one-handed and two-handed), and occasionally the running one-hander. Anything taking place in the air (other than a basic layup) was viewed as being a little crazy. Sailors was not the first to experiment with, or even perfect, this shot, and a dozen more seasons would pass before the jump shot became a common sight in basketball games. The popularity of the "jumper," however, can be traced to Sailors and the 1943 final at Madison Square Garden. By the time he was shipped overseas the following fall, every kid in the country was experimenting with it.

The eastern half of the draw pitted DePaul against Georgetown. The Blue Demons were the talk of Chicago with their star center, George Mikan. The toughest, meanest big man around, he could not be controlled one-on-one. Mikan came to DePaul unskilled and uncoordinated, but coach Ray Meyer spent endless hours working on every phase of his game. A sophomore in 1943, Mikan was just beginning to make a name for himself. He had a couple of talented teammates in Jimmy Cominsky and John Jorgensen, but the Blue Demons had not quite fused as a team. Georgetown had the kind of squad that could take DePaul—the Hoyas were smart, slick passers and had a pretty big center of their own, John Mahnken.

DePaul outplayed Georgetown in the first half and appeared to be in good shape when Mahnken had to leave the game with foul trouble. Then the Hoyas' quickness began to turn the tide. Every time Mikan swiveled his hulking frame one way, a Hoya would dart the other way. Whenever he challenged to block a shot, a cutter snuck in

behind him. It was a marvelous offensive display by Coach Elmer Ripley's team, which defeated the Blue Demons 53-49.

In the western final, Sailors dueled Texas's John Hargis. The Longhorns' sharpshooter made 17 of his team's first 26 points and finished with 29 for the game. Sailors made fewer baskets but outplayed Hargis in every other phase of the game as the Cowboys mounted a stirring comeback. While Texas concentrated on chasing down Sailors, center Milo Koemnich and reserve Jimmy Collins picked up the slack and led the team to a 58-54 win.

The championship game was an exciting affair. Wyoming started strong, with Koemnich, Sailors, and Jim Weir penetrating the Georgetown perimeter for short shots. The Hoyas, led by playmaker Danny Kraus, came back and had a slim lead at halftime. In the second half, Georgetown extended its lead to 31-26 with about 7 minutes left. Kraus and forward Dan Gabbianelli were in foul trouble, however, and this kept the Hoyas from being aggressive down the stretch. At this point, Sailors took over. He ran the Wyoming offense beautifully, enabling the Cowboys to exploit their size advantage over the Hoyas. Every so often, he would stop and pop one of his trademark jumpers. By the time the smoke cleared, Sailors had led his team on an 11-0 run. The Hoyas mounted one more charge, but Wyoming held them off for a 46-43 victory.

Champion: Wyoming
Winning Coach: Everett Shelton
Number of Schools in Tournament: 8
Best Player: Kenny Sailors, Wyoming

1944

Dartmouth Indians
Iowa State Cyclones
Ohio State Buckeyes
Utah Utes

For many decades, the NCAA forbade freshmen to compete in varsity sports. Among the reasons for this were the academic challenges many first-year students encountered and the size difference between 16-, 17-, and 18-year-olds and upperclassmen, who might be as old as 23 or 24. During World War II, the NCAA had little choice but to let the freshmen play. So many upperclassmen had enlisted in the military that there was not enough manpower left to field varsity teams without using first-year players. The basketball programs that had stocked their teams with freshmen found to their delight that many were quite ready to excel at the varsity level. Utah coach Vadal Peterson, for one, felt as if he had hit the jackpot. Four of his five starters were freshmen—including star forward Arnie Ferrin—while his oldest first-stringer, Fred Sheffield, was a sophomore. With one of the best records in the nation, Utah was invited to play in both the NIT and the NCAA Tournament. Peterson decided to accept the bid from the more prestigious NIT, which offered to pay his team's expenses to New York. When the Utes lost in the first round, they were invited to stop in Kansas City on the way home and try their luck in the NCAA Tournament. The Utes beat Missouri in the first round to advance to the Final Four. They were joined by Dartmouth, Ohio State, and Iowa State.

Utah squared off against Iowa State in the western final. The Cyclones, coached by Louis Menze, led briefly in the first half, then challenged in the second half. In the end, however, Iowa State was overmatched. Whenever its defense stopped one Ute, such as Ferrin, two more seemed to pop up and score. Utah won 40-31, with Sheffield and Japanese-American freshman Wat Misaka hitting big buckets down the stretch.

Dartmouth, the tournament favorite, was one of the few basketball programs that actually benefited from the war. Because a handful of college stars were stationed near campus for naval training, Coach Earl Brown was able to "recruit" Dick McGuire, Bob Gale, and Harry Leggatt to take a course or two at Dartmouth—and thus be eligible to play on his basketball team. It was McGuire's great defense, along with 28 points from Aud Brindley, that enabled Dartmouth to beat Ohio State 60-53. The Buckeyes got 21 points from their big star, Arnie Risen, but the support players just were not there for him.

Given the sorry state of sports in the United States during World War II, the 1944 NCAA Final could have been a landmark event. Utah's furious freshmen versus Dartmouth's Navy recruits had the makings of a fun game. But it did not turn out that way. Whether tired or nervous or both, the two teams fumbled and flopped their way through one of the ugliest first halves of basketball anyone had ever seen. Both schools were missing wide-open shots and losing balls they normally held on to.

Coach Peterson was hoping Ferrin would heat up in the second half, and he did. Brindley, meanwhile, could not reproduce his effort of the previous game. With 2 minutes left, the Utes had a 4-point lead. Gambling that Utah would miss its free throws, Coach Brown ordered the Dartmouth players to foul. Peterson was worried that his freshmen would crack under the pressure. He took advantage of a little-used rule of the era and chose not to accept his foul shots, and instead to keep possession of the ball. This choice proved to be disastrous, as the Indians tied the game on a desperation shot by McGuire with 3 seconds to go.

Both teams played cautiously in overtime, scoring 4 points apiece. With 20 seconds left, Utah had the ball. As time ticked away, Herb Wilkinson, another one of Peterson's freshmen, held the ball beyond the top of the key, looking desperately for somewhere to pass. With all of his team-

mates covered and Dartmouth practically daring him to shoot, Wilkinson did just that—he let fly a high-arcing set shot with a lot of backspin. His long bomb plunked against the rim and stuck there for an instant before dropping through for the championship. The Utes celebrated their 42-40 victory by hopping a train back to New York, where they played the winner of the NIT, St. John's, in a game to benefit the Red Cross. Utah beat the Redmen, and in doing so claimed a bit of college basketball history as the sport's first "unified" champion.

Champion: Utah
Winning Coach: Vadal Peterson
Number of Schools in Tournament: 8
Best Player: Arnie Ferrin, Utah

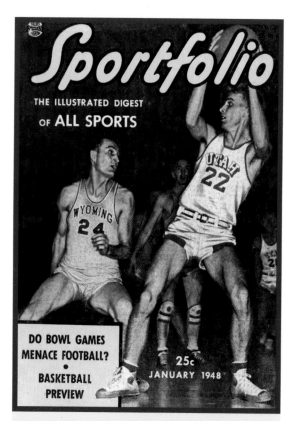

Arnie Ferrin (22) became a national star after leading his team to victory in 1944.

1945
Arkansas Razorbacks
New York University Violets
Ohio State Buckeyes
Oklahoma A&M Aggies

Prior to the 1945 NCAA Tournament, the role of the "big man" in college basketball was still unclear. In a game that rewarded quickness and coordination, there appeared to be no place for slow-moving 7-footers. An occasional brute like DePaul's George Mikan might dominate for a year or two, but he was the exception, not the rule. It seems strange today, but back then no one thought of basketball as a game that could be played above the rim. In fact, after the center jump was abolished, some people predicted that big men would slowly disappear from the game!

Oklahoma A&M's Bob Kurland, who stood 6-foot-11, changed a lot of minds. Nicknamed "Foothills," he had been teased about his size most of his life. Coach Hank Iba and former college star Floyd Burdette worked with Kurland after he arrived on campus in 1942. They taught him how to use his long arms and strong legs to dominate the middle and to alter the flow of the game. It took a full season (during which the big man averaged a paltry 2.5 points per game), but in time Iba was able to build a team and a game plan around Kurland.

Iba surrounded Kurland with darting shooters and ballhandlers like Cecil Hankins and Doyle Parrack. With their center able to overwhelm most opponents, the Aggies reached the Final Four with ease in 1945. In the western final, Arkansas tried packing a zone defense around Kurland. This left A&M's outside shooters wide open, and they made their shots. On the defensive end, Kurland neutralized Razorbacks center George Kok and shut down the driving lanes to the basket. Forced to attempt long-range shots, Arkansas fell behind and eventually lost, 68-41.

On the other side of the draw, Ohio State's 6-foot-9 Arnie Risen faced off against NYU's 16-year-old freshman, 6-foot-8 Dolph Schayes. Both pivot men would go on to Hall of Fame pro careers, but in this contest Risen was the teacher and Schayes the student. The Buckeyes built on a slim halftime lead, as Risen poured in 26 points to give his team a 10-point advantage. Then the All-American fouled out with 2 minutes left, and this left a window open for the Violets. After his players scored 6 quick points, NYU coach Howard Cann instructed them to foul Ohio State. The Buckeyes missed their free throws, the

Cecil Hankins and Hank Iba chat during the 1945 tournament. Led by Bob Kurland, the Aggies won the title.

Violets tied the score and then prevailed in overtime, 70-65.

Cann figured his best chance to beat A&M in the final was to employ a full-court press. This would limit Kurland's involvement in the offense. Expecting this strategy, Iba told his players to be patient. This they did, slowly working the ball into the frontcourt and waiting for Kurland to establish position. The Violets were able to intercept enough passes to keep the game close, but in the end Kurland was just too much for young Schayes. Kurland scored 22 points and grabbed almost as many rebounds. The man called "Foothills" was a mountain of trouble, and A&M won the game 49-45.

> **Champion: Oklahoma A&M**
> Winning Coach: Hank Iba
> Number of Schools in Tournament: 8
> Best Player: Bob Kurland,
> Oklahoma A&M

1946
California Golden Bears
North Carolina Tar Heels
Ohio State Buckeyes
Oklahoma A&M Aggies

One year older and one year wiser, Oklahoma A&M's Bob Kurland was looking to take his game one level higher in the 1946 Final Four. With Cecil Hankins and Doyle Parrack graduated, forward Sam Aubrey became Kurland's chief accomplice. Aubrey was one of many returning veterans who had taken time off from college to fight in World War II. He had been wounded in battle, and for a time doctors had thought he might not walk again.

California, coached by Nibs Price, had a dynamic duo of its own in Andy Wolfe and Merv Lafaille. The Tar Heels, coached by Ben Carnevale, also boasted a talented tandem in John Dillon and Horace "Bones" McKinney, a deadly hook-shot artist who could score with either hand. The Buckeyes remained the cream of the crop in the Big Ten despite the loss of their two best players, Arnie Risen and Don Grate. After some academic difficulties, Risen had decided to sign a pro contract with the Indianapolis Kautskys of the National Basketball League. Grate had also decided to go pro, having signed as a baseball pitcher with the Philadelphia Phillies in the spring of 1945.

Oklahoma A&M won easily over California, 52-35, in the western final. The victory made the Aggies the first team ever to repeat as champions in the West. The key was Kurland, who was unstoppable. Knowing that the Golden Bears had no one who could guard his center effectively, Hank Iba told the Aggies to dump the ball into the post all game long. Kurland poured in 29 points—many on jarring dunks—and outscored Lafaille and Wolfe, who combined for just 11 baskets.

In the eastern final, Ohio State suffered a heartbreaking loss for the second year in a row. The Buckeyes started the game slowly but managed to take a 20-19 lead by halftime. Center Jack Underman was handling

After bringing UNC within 3 points of the championship in 1946, Bones McKinney became a pro star. He returned to the Final Four as a coach with Wake Forest in 1962.

McKinney well, and the UNC center eventually fouled out with just nine points. The Tar Heels fought back, however, and whittled 5 points off of Ohio State's 7-point lead with 20 seconds to go. North Carolina forward Bob Paxton, standing 30 feet from the hoop, tossed up a high-arcing set shot that seemed to hang in the air forever. It found nothing but net, and for the second straight year the Buckeyes found themselves in an unexpected overtime battle. The Tar Heels outscored Ohio State 6-3 in the extra period to advance to the championship game.

In the final, Coach Carnevale decided to deal with Kurland by harassing him every time he touched the ball. This strategy got McKinney, Paxton, and Jim Jordan into foul trouble and did little to rattle the Aggies. Kurland simply powered to the basket or fired passes to open teammates.

Trailing by 13 early in the second half, UNC switched tactics and began pressuring the other A&M players. This worked better. Dillon spearheaded a comeback, and the Tar Heels pulled to within three points of the Aggies. Sensing the game slipping from his team's grasp, Kurland demanded the ball on back-to-back possessions. Both times he wheeled to the hoop and dunked over the Carolina defenders. Although the score remained close, A&M prevailed 43-40. Kurland, with 23 points, had many people whispering that basketball would soon become a big man's game.

> **Champion: Oklahoma A&M**
> **Winning Coach: Hank Iba**
> **Number of Schools in Tournament: 8**
> **Best Player: Bob Kurland,**
> **Oklahoma A&M**

1947
City College of New York Beavers
Holy Cross Crusaders
Oklahoma Sooners
Texas Longhorns

During the first eight years of the NCAA Tournament, western schools had done extremely well against their eastern rivals. Everyone had an idea why this was so. Some said that East Coast basketball was inferior to the styles developing elsewhere. Others pointed to the fact that the richer NIT often attracted the top eastern colleges, which left second-tier schools to play in the newer event. The presence of Holy Cross in the 1947 Final Four proved both theories wrong.

Coach Alvin "Doggie" Julian built his team out of New York City playground stars, including playmaker Joe Mullaney and center George Kaftan. These players were quick, they were smart, and they knew how to work mismatches in their favor. CCNY also featured a team of top New Yorkers, including high-scoring Irwin Dambrot. The Beavers were a fast-breaking club that pressured opponents into mistakes. The western teams in the Final Four were Texas, another fast-break-oriented squad, and Oklahoma, a hard-nosed defensive team led by All-American center Gerry Tucker.

In the eastern final, CCNY tested Holy Cross from the opening tip. Coach Nat Holman—one of the game's all-time greats—implored his players to push the ball up the court. This resulted in many easy baskets and an early 11-point lead. Holy Cross's defense regrouped and shut down CCNY's running game, while Kaftan proved unstoppable on offense. He scored 19 points in the first half, enabling the Crusaders to regain the lead by halftime, 27-25. The second half belonged to Holy Cross, which won 60-45.

In the western final, shifty Slater Martin of the Longhorns gave the Sooners fits as Texas surged to a 7-point halftime lead. In the second period, Tucker took over at both ends with his rebounding and passing. With 10 seconds left, Oklahoma only trailed by a point. The ball went to Tucker, who whipped a perfect pass to wide-open Ken Pryor, and Pryor—who had not made a basket all game—sank the long-range shot to give the Sooners a 55-54 victory.

In the final, Tucker's continued good play caused Kaftan to struggle in the first

half, and Oklahoma took a 31-28 lead. In the locker room, Coach Julian told his Crusaders to pick up the pace. He also put forward Bob Curran on Tucker so that Kaftan could get a breather. Both moves worked, and Holy Cross quickly regained the lead. Kaftan finally heated up and finished with 18 points. Fellow Crusaders Dermie O'Connell and Frank Oftring swarmed all over the Sooners and added 30 more points. The game ended 58-47, and with it all talk of the inferiority of eastern basketball ended, too.

Champion: Holy Cross
Winning Coach: Doggie Julian
Number of Schools in Tournament: 8
Best Player: George Kaftan,
           Holy Cross

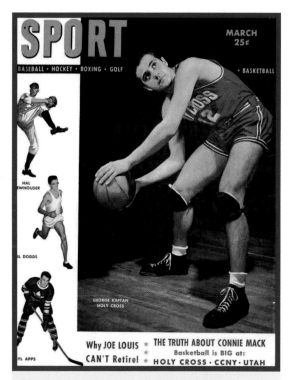

Towering George Kaftan had to crouch in order to fit on this cover of *Sport* **magazine. He stood tall against Oklahoma in the NCAA final.**

1948
Baylor Bears
Holy Cross Crusaders
Kansas State Wildcats
Kentucky Wildcats

The 1948 Final Four marked the return of the Kentucky Wildcats to NCAA Tournament play. Adolph Rupp had elected to compete solely in the NIT in 1946 and 1947, but in 1948 he planned to play in both events. That was good news for the tournament. The Wildcats had six of the world's best players—college or pro—and a coach who knew how to keep them winning and happy. The team's frontcourt was made up of Alex Groza, Cliff Barker, and Wallace "Wah Wah" Jones. Groza, the top player in college ball that year, was the brother of Lou Groza, the star tackle and placekicker

Alex Groza, the star of stars for Adolph Rupp's Kentucky Wildcats. He was twice named the tournament's top player.

for the champion Cleveland Browns. The 6-foot-7 center was a World War II veteran, as was Barker. Jones was a multitalented forward who could score, rebound, and defend. Guard Ralph Beard ran the offense with help from Kenny Rollins and Joe Holland. It was said that when Rupp split up these six in practice, he had the two best teams in the country.

The other schools in the Final Four were just that—"other" schools. It looked like no one could beat Kentucky. Baylor, coached by Bill Henderson, relied on an offense that sped down the court at breakneck speed. Bill Johnson and Don Heatherington were the Bears' best players. Holy Cross, the defending national champion, had George Kaftan and sophomore playmaker Bob Cousy, who was now the team's point guard. Cousy's dribbling and passing skills were sensational, but without a strong supporting cast he was often forced to do too much on his own. The fourth team, Kansas State, had a well-balanced but unspectacular lineup featuring Rick Harman. These teams were good, but Kentucky was great.

In the eastern final, Kentucky shut down Cousy and fouled him out, and Kaftan managed just six baskets for the Crusaders. Meanwhile, Groza scored 23 in an easy 60-52 win. In the western final, Baylor and Kansas State fought for the right to get creamed by the Wildcats in the title game. This semifinal was a close contest until late in the second half, when Heatherington converted a bunch of free throws. Baylor won, also by the score of 60-52.

Going into the championship, the Bears knew they could not play inside with Kentucky. Coach Henderson decided to gamble on his team's outside shooting, but Kentucky was not even giving up 25-footers. The smothering defense of the Wildcats resulted in a 12-point lead just 8 minutes into the game. The final score was 58-42, with everyone contributing to the winning cause.

Champion: Kentucky
Winning Coach: Adolph Rupp
Number of Schools in Tournament: 8
Best Player: Alex Groza, Kentucky

1949
Illinois Fighting Illini
Kentucky Wildcats
Oklahoma A&M Aggies
Oregon State Beavers

For the second year in a row, it appeared the Final Four was just a formality before the Kentucky Wildcats would be crowned kings of college basketball. Alex Groza, Ralph Beard, and Wah Wah Jones were back, and the team had seemed unbeatable all year. The glimmer of hope for Kentucky's opponents lay in two curious losses. The veteran players had all mysteriously unraveled in the final moments of a game against the University of St. Louis back in December. In the NIT, the same thing had happened. Kentucky's first Final Four opponent would be Illinois, the Big Ten Conference champ. Assuming that game went well, the Wildcats would face either Oregon State or Oklahoma A&M, which had a very tall starting five.

In the eastern final, the Wildcats were sharp against Illinois in a 76-47 blowout. They converted baskets in the open court with their fast break and beat the Illini in the half-court game thanks to Groza, who scored 27 points. Oklahoma A&M crushed Oregon State in the western final, 55-30. Bob Harris, A&M's skinny center, hit eight shots from the paint and added seven free throws.

The final featured a clash between two great coaches playing two completely different styles. Adolph Rupp liked to steamroll Kentucky's enemies with an aggressive, athletic game. Hank Iba preferred to loop a defensive "noose" around opponents and then to tighten it slowly. Early in the contest, it looked like Iba's boys might pull off an upset; the Aggies' patience paid off, and they took the lead. Rupp countered by ordering the Wildcats to match A&M's defensive effort. The two teams fought to a standstill until the second half, when the powerful Groza caused Harris to foul out with 16 minutes left. That was it for A&M. With no one to stop Groza, Iba watched helplessly as his Aggies fell 46-36.

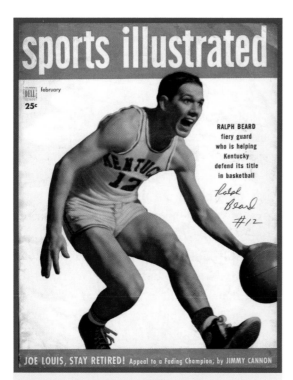

Ralph Beard, the floor leader of the Wildcats, was one of the most famous athletes in the United States during the late 1940s.

Champion: Kentucky
Winning Coach: Adolph Rupp
Number of Schools in Tournament: 8
Best Player: Alex Groza, Kentucky

THE 1950s

1950

Baylor Bears
Bradley Braves
North Carolina State Wolfpack
City College of New York Beavers

The NCAA Tournament had a new look in 1950 thanks to CCNY. For the first time, African-Americans appeared in the starting lineup of a Final Four team. Coach Nat Holman had been recruiting black players for a few years, and he came up with three terrific ones in Floyd Lane, Joe Galiber, and Ed Warner. Lane was an excellent all-around guard, and Galiber a defensive whirlwind at center. Warner was the team's second-leading scorer behind Irwin Dambrot, who had blossomed into a major star. Although CCNY had just won the prestigious NIT over Bradley and its hot-shooting star Gene Melchiorre, there were no guarantees they would fare as well in the Final Four. North Carolina State had an explosive offense led by All-Americans Dick Dickey and Sam Ranzino; Baylor still had Don Heatherington; and Bradley, still considered by many to be the nation's best team, was also lying in wait.

In the eastern final, NC State's offense stalled against CCNY when guard Vic Bubas left the game with a bad ankle. The

Wolfpack stayed close, but late in the second half, Ranzino and Dickey fouled out, and the Beavers eked out a 78-73 win. The western final was a seesaw battle, too. In the first half, the muscular Heatherington kept the Bears within striking range, and only 3

A Bradley player corrals a loose ball in first-half action from the 1950 championship game. CCNY's Ed Warner watches at far left.

points separated the teams at halftime. The Braves and the Bears traded baskets for 10 minutes in the second half until a couple of substitutes got hot for Bradley and sparked the team to a 68-66 win.

The NCAA Final was a return match between Bradley and CCNY—once again played before a packed house in New York City's Madison Square Garden. With their fans chanting the school cheer, the Beavers drew first blood on the shooting of long-distance specialist Norman Mager. After being knocked unconscious in an on-court collision, Mager returned to the game in the second half. This forced Bradley coach Forddy Anderson to abandon his zone defense and play man-to-man. A last-minute scoring flurry by Melchiorre drew the Braves to within a point, and then Melchiorre stole a pass and streaked toward the CCNY basket. Dambrot, running all the way, caught up with him and tipped the layup. He then fired a long pass to Mager, who hit the shot that put the game on ice. CCNY claimed the first official double championship, 71-68.

Kentucky star Cliff Hagan went on to enjoy a Hall of Fame career in the NBA. His cards are still in great demand by collectors.

> **Champion: City College (NY)**
> **Winning Coach: Nat Holman**
> **Number of Schools in Tournament: 8**
> **Best Player: Irwin Dambrot, CCNY**

1951
Illinois Fighting Illini
Kansas State Wildcats
Kentucky Wildcats
Oklahoma A&M Aggies

For the second time in three seasons, the NCAA championship looked like it would be a contest between Kentucky and Okla-

homa A&M. But looks can be deceiving. With the field expanded from 8 schools to 16, the road to the Final Four was now twice as long. Still, the Wildcats and the Aggies made it. Adolph Rupp had an entirely new squad, led by sophomore forwards Frank Ramsey and Cliff Hagan. Ramsey was what today is called a "point forward." He, not the Kentucky guards, initiated the offense. Hagan, who stood just 6-foot-4, played power forward and center. He had an amazing hook shot that was impossible to block. Opponents dared not put a 7-footer on Ha-

SCANDALS OF '51

Adolph Rupp told the players on the great Kentucky teams of the 1940s that the only way they could lose was if they "beat themselves." How right he was. During the 1950–51 season, police began investigating rumors that well-known players had been losing games on purpose for many years. The authorities uncovered a widespread conspiracy that shook the squeaky-clean world of college basketball.

When the smoke cleared, it was proved that 30 top players had fixed the outcomes of more than 80 games in 20 cities between 1947 and 1950.

Among those implicated were three of the nation's most glamorous basketball programs and three of the biggest coaches—Bradley (Forddy Anderson), CCNY (Nat Holman), and Kentucky (Rupp). Among the players caught in the investigation were stars Alex Groza, Ralph Beard, Gene Melchiorre, and Sherman White. The plot, hatched in New York City, had involved many of the schools that visited Madison Square Garden to compete in the prestigious NIT. It certainly explained a lot of bizarre losses, particularly those by Kentucky.

The scandal destroyed college basketball in New York and forever tarnished the reputation of the NIT. The NCAA, which had held its tournament final in New York seven times since 1943, did not schedule postseason games in that city for four decades. Later, the NCAA made it a rule that all conference champions had to enter the NCAA Tournament, and this crippled the NIT even more.

If there was a winner in this mess, it was the fledgling NBA, which instantly banned every player who had been caught in the scandal. A "poor sister" to college ball for many decades, it gained thousands of new fans, who no longer believed that NCAA basketball was "on the level."

gan because that would have left the Wildcats' 7-footer, Bill Spivey, to roam the lane at will. Kentucky roared through its schedule with just two losses.

Oklahoma A&M also had a superb team. As always, the Aggies were tough on defense. Illinois, Big Ten champion once again, was led by Don Sunderlage and Rod Fletcher. Kansas State had a balanced attack that was well coached by Jack Gardner.

Illinois put Kentucky to the test in the eastern final. Fletcher and Sunderlage dev-astated the Wildcats' defense to give the Illini a 39-32 lead at the half. Rupp had some choice words for his players, especially the towering Spivey, who had been nearly invisible. The gangly center responded with a huge second half to finish with 29 points and 16 rebounds. Spivey fouled out with 3 minutes left, but Kentucky had regained the lead. With 29 seconds left, Illinois managed to tie the game. Ramsey responded for Kentucky with a great pass to teammate Shelby Linville, who hit a short jump shot. In the final seconds, Sunderlage took the ball the length of the court for Illinois and threw up a shot at the buzzer. It missed, and Kentucky advanced to face Kansas State in the finals with a 76-74 triumph. State had upset Hank Iba's A&M team 68-44, thanks to a superb game from Lew Hitch.

For the second time in tournament history, two colleges with the same team nickname (Wildcats) met for the championship. Kansas State was a big underdog but held out hope for a victory nevertheless. A few weeks earlier they had thrashed Illinois—the same team that nearly had defeated Kentucky. By beating Rupp's players to loose balls and rebounds, Kansas State managed to play Kentucky even for a half. Then the sleeping giant, Spivey, awoke in the second half. During a crucial 8-minute span, Kansas State went scoreless while Spivey dumped in six shots. From there, it was easy. Kentucky had its third championship in four years, 68-58.

> **Champion: Kentucky**
> **Winning Coach: Adolph Rupp**
> **Number of Schools in Tournament: 16**
> **Best Player: Bill Spivey, Kentucky**

1952
Illinois Fighting Illini
Kansas Jayhawks
Santa Clara Broncos
St. John's Redmen

Phog Allen was running out of time. According to school policy, the 66-year-old Kansas coach would face mandatory retirement in just a few years. His last chance for a championship in the tournament he helped to create was Clyde Lovellette. And as last chances go, Lovellette was a big one. At 6-foot-9 (and 240 pounds), he dwarfed most college centers. Unlike most big men, however, "Cumulus Clyde" moved well and had a silky shooting touch. The senior led the nation in scoring with 28.4 points per game and pulled down 10 to 20 rebounds a night. Poised to stop this force of nature in the Final Four were Johnny Kerr of Illinois, Bob Zawoluk of St. John's, and Kenny Sears of Santa Clara.

Santa Clara was the first victim. The Broncos had already played the role of David twice in the tournament by upsetting two Goliaths—UCLA and Wyoming. This time, when they collapsed their defense around Lovellette, Kansas guards Dean Kelley and Charlie Hoag made them pay by hitting long set shots. The Jayhawks stretched their 13-point halftime advantage to 19 in a 74-55 win. Lovellette was the high scorer with 33.

St. John's, which had shocked a tough Kentucky squad to reach the Final Four, edged Illinois 61-59. The difference in the game was the 6-foot-9 Zawoluk, who scored 24 points and made several key shots for the Redmen in the final minutes.

The two NCAA finalists in 1952 had a strategic advantage over past tournament teams. For the first time, the Final Four participants had all played in one place (Seattle), so the coaches could actually scout their next opponent. Since 1940, the western half of the draw had been decided in Kansas City; the eastern half had been played in New York since 1943. Thus, the 1952 NCAA Tournament marked the first Final Four as fans know it today.

Having watched Lovellette in person,

St. John's coach Frank McGuire felt Zawoluk could score on him, but he would have trouble defending him. Rather than double-teaming the Kansas pivot man, McGuire instructed his players to make life miserable for the rest of the Jayhawks with a relentless full-court press. Although McGuire had watched the Jayhawks in action, his strategy was not effective. For every steal they made, the Redmen also allowed a wide-open layup. The Jayhawks built a double-digit lead in the first half and put the game away when Zawoluk fouled out in the second half. Lovellette hit for 33 points again, and Kansas gave Coach Allen his championship by a score of 80-63.

Champion: Kansas
Winning Coach: Phog Allen
Number of Schools in Tournament: 16
Best Player: Clyde Lovellette, Kansas

1953
Indiana Hoosiers
Kansas Jayhawks
Louisiana State Tigers
Washington Huskies

Defense wins championships. It is true today, and it was true back in 1953, even though scoring was way up during the season. More than ever, basketball was being played in the air, above the rim, and on the run. As a result, the all-time team scoring mark of 82.5 points per game was broken by no fewer than eight colleges during the year. When it came down to the Final Four, however, just about everyone agreed that defense would rule the day. This made Indiana one of the tournament favorites. Coach Branch McCracken had assembled a team that was as good at stopping the fast break as running the fast break. The Hoosiers were led by sophomore center Don Schlundt and junior

After their performance in the 1953 tournament, Don Schlundt and Slick Leonard were easy picks for the cover of the 1954 NCAA record book.

guard Slick Leonard—together known as "Mr. Inside and Mr. Outside."

Indiana's chief rival would be Kansas, set to defend its championship without Clyde Lovellette, who had graduated. The best players in the draw were LSU junior Bob Pettit and Washington senior Bob Houbregs. Both were typical of the new breed of college scorer. Big and mobile, they could stretch defenses with their outside shooting, then penetrate to the hoop when opponents came out to guard them.

In the first semifinal, Pettit was no match for Indiana's two stars. Schlundt and Leonard combined for 51 points, and the Hoosiers simply overwhelmed LSU, 80-67. Defense was more of a factor in the second game. Worn down by the Kansas press, the Washington Huskies never found their rhythm and fell 79-53. Lovellette's successor, Bob Born, scored 25 points for the Jayhawks.

The big stories of the championship game were the off-court duel between masterminds Allen and McCracken and the on-court competition between Leonard and Kansas's sharpshooting Dean Kelley. With the final staged in Kansas City, the Jayhawks were given a slight edge in this epic battle. From the opening tip, the game got tighter and tighter. The stars fought each other to a draw in the first half, which enabled several bench players to step up and contribute. Indiana and Kansas were knotted 41-41 at intermission.

In the second half, the defenses took over and scoring plunged. Born fouled out, but the exhausted Schlundt made little progress against Born's replacement, Jerry Alberts. With 27 seconds left and the game tied, Leonard was fouled. The junior stepped to the line and hit one of two free throws to give Indiana a 69-68 lead. Coach Allen called time-out and told his players to hold for the final shot. When play resumed, the fans watched breathlessly as the Jayhawks prepared to try for the game-winner. Unable to find an open shooter, Kansas threw the ball to Alberts in the corner. As time ticked away, the terrified backup center squeezed off a desperate shot. It clanked off the rim as the buzzer sounded, and Indiana was the new NCAA champion.

Champion: Indiana
Winning Coach: Branch McCracken
Number of Schools in Tournament: 22
Best Player: Bob Born, Kansas

1954
Bradley Braves
La Salle Explorers
Penn State Nittany Lions
Southern California Trojans

Although fewer than half of today's 64 teams were being invited to the NCAA Tournament in the mid-1950s, there was always a handful of "Cinderella" teams to root for—underdogs who squeak into the draw before being squashed by the larger programs. In 1954, three such teams survived to make it all the way to the Final Four: Bradley, Penn State, and Southern California. The fourth college, La Salle, was hardly a powerhouse—the Explorers were not even ranked in the Top 10. The Explorers squeaked in when top-rated Kentucky declined a tournament bid, second-ranked Indiana lost its opening game, and the nation's 3-4-5 teams decided to take their chances in the NIT instead.

Most agreed that La Salle was the class of this Final Four. The school's leading player, Tom Gola, was one of the new breed of basketball stars who could create his own scoring opportunities and play above the rim. He was almost impossible to stop. Bradley, under coach Forddy Anderson, had been in this spot before. The Braves were led by high-scoring Bob Carney and Dick Estergard. Penn State advanced on the strength of coach Elmer Gross's confusing defensive schemes and the fine all-around

play of athletic center Jesse Arnelle. USC's Roy Irvin had a great tournament, as the Trojans survived a double-overtime thriller to reach the Final Four.

In the first game, Penn State gave La Salle a scare when Arnelle neutralized Gola and held him to just nine shots. Explorers coach Ken Loeffler asked sophomore forwards Charlie Singley and Frank Blatcher to pick up the slack, and they responded with a combined 29 points. La Salle cruised to an easy 69-54 win. In the second game, Dick Welsh and Roy Irvin helped the Trojans build a 10-point lead, but Bradley crept back midway through the second half. A late charge sparked by Carney put the

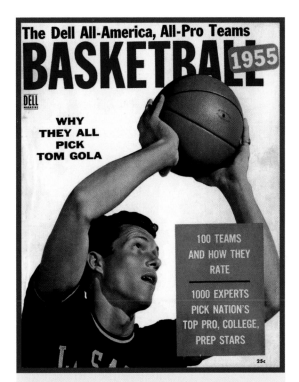

The first basketball-only magazines started hitting the newsstands in the early 1950s, thanks to sensational scorers like Tom Gola.

Braves in front, and they held on for a 74-72 victory.

The NCAA Final pitted the up-tempo Braves against the methodical Explorers, who looked for Gola almost every time down the court. In the early going, Bradley seemed a step faster and opened up a nice lead. La Salle managed to slow the pace down and drew to within a point by halftime. In the locker room, Loeffler gambled on a strategy that he hoped would catch Bradley off guard. He told his troops to come out running and gunning in the second half. The Braves did not know what hit them when the plodding Explorers were suddenly swarming all over the court. Again, Singley and Blatcher made the difference. When Bradley double-teamed Gola, they found open shots and made them, combining for 46 points. A tight game became a runaway, and La Salle took the title with a 92-76 win.

> **Champion: La Salle**
> **Winning Coach: Ken Loeffler**
> **Number of Schools in Tournament: 24**
> **Best Player: Tom Gola, La Salle**

1955
Colorado Buffaloes
Iowa Hawkeyes
La Salle Explorers
San Francisco Dons

Tom Gola and La Salle returned to the Final Four after winning it all in 1954. This time they were headed for a showdown with a new and frightening force: a center who dominated in the paint and ran the floor like a guard. His name was Bill Russell, and he teamed with guard K.C. Jones to make the San Francisco Dons practically unbeatable. These two defensive geniuses operated on the theory that if you did not allow your man to shoot, there was no way he could score. Thus, in an era when 90- and 100-point games were increasingly common, the Dons regularly held opponents to 10 baskets or fewer per half. The two other teams involved in the Final Four were Colorado, which relied on the strong play of center Burdette Halderson, and Iowa, led by high-scoring Bill Logan.

As expected, Russell ate Halderson alive. The Colorado big man fouled out just 6 minutes into the second half, and the Buffaloes fell 62-50. In the other semifinal, Logan and company gave La Salle a run for its money. Despite a big offensive game from Gola, the Explorers could not halt Iowa's balanced attack. La Salle barely won, 76-73. It was the team's first tough game of the tournament, but it could not have come at a worse time.

Fresh off their defeat of Colorado, the Dons were ready for exhausted La Salle. San Francisco coach Phil Woolpert surprised the experts by asking Jones to guard Gola. Though a half-foot shorter, Jones was such a smart defensive player that he handled Gola with ease. Free to roam the lane on defense, Russell swatted away layup after layup and pulled in a staggering number of rebounds. His outlet passes ignited the San Francisco fast break, and often he was the man who finished, sprinting down the court past bewildered opponents to dunk the ball. The Dons built an 11-point lead by halftime, then snuffed out La Salle's various comeback attempts in the final 20 minutes. Russell and Jones finished with 23 points each, and San Francisco won 77-63.

USF fans hoist Bill Russell onto their shoulders after the Dons defeated La Salle in 1955.

Champion: San Francisco
Winning Coach: Phil Woolpert
Number of Schools in Tournament: 24
Best Player: Bill Russell, San Francisco

1956
Iowa Hawkeyes
San Francisco Dons
Southern Methodist Mustangs
Temple Owls

By the 1956 Final Four, the Dons of San Francisco were a monster of a team. Bill Russell had become the best shot-blocker and rebounder anyone had ever seen. His supporting cast—K.C. Jones, Hal Perry, and Gene Brown—were excellent players, too. They finished the 1955–1956 season with a 25-0 record and headed into the Final Four having won 51 games in a row over two seasons. Not one of the other three teams stood a chance, claimed the sportswriters.

Iowa, SMU, and Temple believed otherwise. Each had good players. Temple's Hal Lear and Guy Rodgers were terrific guards; SMU's Jim Krebs was a top center; and Iowa had all of its best players back from the year before, when they nearly toppled La Salle in the Final Four. But what gave these schools the most hope was that San Francisco would be without Jones. He had redshirted the 1953–1954 season after having an appendectomy, and the rules stated that a fifth-year senior could not compete in tournament play.

In the first game, Carl Logan scored at will against Temple, but the Iowa center was powerless to stop Lear and Rodgers, who were making 4 out of every 5 baskets for the Owls. Iowa managed to maintain a

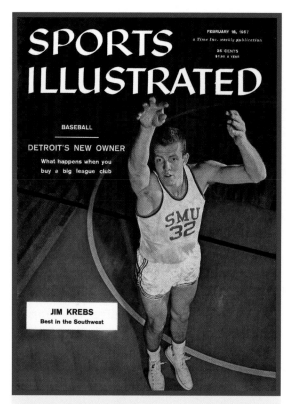

Sports Illustrated's first college basketball cover featured Jim Krebs of SMU. He was the only player able to keep Bill Russell in check.

court. Farmer finished with a game-high 26 points to give the Dons an 86-68 win.

No one stepped up for the Dons early in the championship game. An astonished crowd watched as Iowa built a 15-4 lead. Hoping to avoid panic, Woolpert kept telling his players to relax and play their game. To his relief, things began to click with a few minutes left in the first half. Perry and Brown began sinking their outside shots, and Russell started working over Logan. The Dons roared back and went into the locker room with a 38-33 lead at the half. The final 20 minutes was all San Francisco—or, rather, all Russell. After a slow start, he finished with 26 points and 27 rebounds, and for the second year in a row San Francisco was the NCAA champion.

> **Champion: San Francisco**
> **Winning Coach: Phil Woolpert**
> **Number of Schools in Tournament: 25**
> **Best Player: Hal Lear, Temple**

slim lead throughout the game and held on to win 83-76.

In the second game, Krebs hustled and took smart shots for SMU, and on defense he prevented Russell from wrecking the Mustangs. This was Coach Doc Hayes's plan. With Krebs playing Russell to a standstill and K.C. Jones sitting in the stands, Hayes hoped someone else would step up and make the difference. Instead, it was one of Phil Woolpert's sophomores who came through. Forward Mike Farmer burned the Mustangs for a couple of early buckets and gained more confidence with each minute on the

1957
Kansas Jayhawks
Michigan State Spartans
North Carolina Tar Heels
San Francisco Dons

When Bill Russell left college after the 1956 Final Four, it was predicted he would dominate other NBA centers. It was also said that he would only have a couple of years at the top. An even more extraordinary player, Kansas's Wilt Chamberlain, was on the horizon. Although he never allowed himself to be measured, it was believed that "Wilt the Stilt" was probably about 7-foot-2. He was very coordinated and had great leaping ability. In fact, when Chamberlain was in high school a rule had to be passed to keep him from dunking his foul shots! Kansas went into the NCAA Tournament as an overwhelming favorite, with Chamberlain often scoring 30 to 40 points and grabbing 20 to 30 rebounds per game.

The Jayhawks had little concern about two of the other Final Four teams. Neither San Francisco nor Michigan State would be able to beat them, although the Spartans figured to give the North Carolina Tar Heels a good game. The UNC squad was a good one. Nicknamed the "Carolina Yankees," the team was coached by New Yorker Frank McGuire and starred five New York City starters:

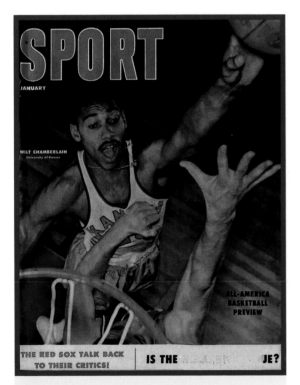

This *Sport* magazine gave fans an idea of how dominant Kansas star Wilt Chamberlain could be.

Lennie Rosenbluth, Pete Brennan, Joe Quigg, Tommy Kearns, and Bobby Cunningham. They had the blend of street-smarts and skill needed to topple the Jayhawks.

Few were surprised when Kansas crushed San Francisco in the semifinal. Without Russell and K.C. Jones, the defending champions had little to offer in the way of resistance. The final score was 80-56, with Chamberlain dominating the entire second half. The Carolina-Michigan State game was a classic. Sparked by the scoring of Rosenbluth and the rebounding of Brennan and Cunningham, the Tar Heels barely held off the hard-charging Spartans, who were led by Johnny Green. State actually had the game won when Jack Quiggle sank a 50-footer at the end of regulation, but the referees ruled that the shot had left his fingers an instant after the final buzzer sounded. It took three overtimes before the Tar Heels finally prevailed, 74-70.

After such a draining battle, few expected UNC to put up a fight against the big, bad Jayhawks in the NCAA Final. Even the fact that Carolina was undefeated for the season did not impress the experts. But Coach McGuire had a plan. He would have at least three of his players guard Chamberlain at all times. If Kansas wanted to force the ball in to its center, that was fine, but the passes would have to be perfect. If they moved the ball quickly, the Jayhawks could get wide-open 15-footers. McGuire was betting they could not make those shots. He knew that sometimes it was easier to score with a defender in your face than with no one on you, and the entire world expecting you to make your shot.

The fans knew something was up when Kearns, the shortest Tar Heel starter, came out to contest the opening tip-off against Chamberlain. As McGuire had hoped, the

Kansas players were not feeding the ball to Chamberlain—and were also missing most of their shots. The Tar Heels opened up a 12-point lead, but the Jayhawks whittled it down to 7 points by the end of the first half. Kansas caught UNC and went ahead with 10 minutes left in the second half. In a controversial move, Jayhawks coach Dick Harp instructed his players to slow down the pace and protect their lead. This enabled the Carolina players to catch their breath, and they chipped away until the game was tied 46-46 at the end of regulation.

Each team scored once in the first overtime, and neither team scored in the second. With 20 seconds left in the third OT, a careless foul by the Jayhawks sent Quigg to the line. He sank both free throws to put UNC ahead, 54-53. With one chance left to win the game, Kansas forced the ball in to Chamberlain. The pass was not high enough, and Quigg tipped it to Kearns, who ran out the clock on an amazing upset win.

> **Champion: North Carolina**
> **Winning Coach: Frank McGuire**
> **Number of Schools in Tournament: 23**
> **Best Player: Wilt Chamberlain, Kansas**

1958
Kansas State Wildcats
Kentucky Wildcats
Seattle Chieftains
Temple Owls

The rebuilding of the Kentucky basketball program was moving along nicely by the 1957–1958 season. After betting scandals and other serious violations ruined Adolph Rupp's reputation, he had found it hard to recruit superstar players. So no one was more surprised than Rupp when the Wildcats reached the Final Four in 1958; he even admitted later that he thought this was as far as his boys would go.

The other three schools had good teams with great players. Temple had an unstoppable scorer in guard Guy Rodgers; Kansas State had a 6-foot-8 whirlwind named Bob Boozer; and Seattle had Elgin Baylor, one of the most outrageous talents college basketball had ever seen. Kentucky's best players were Adrian Smith, Vern Hatton, and Johnny Cox—hardly household names in a tournament that also featured All-Americans (and future pro stars) Oscar Robertson, Jerry West, Rudy La Russo, and Wayne Embry.

In the first semifinal, Kentucky got to know Temple again. Earlier in the year, the two schools had played three overtimes before Kentucky had pulled out a narrow victory. Good defense and poor shooting characterized their Final Four meeting, which also went down to the wire. Late in the second half, Rodgers had the ball with a one-point lead, knowing he would be fouled if he got anywhere near the basket. As expected, Kentucky sent him to the line. The normally dependable Rodgers missed his shot, and the Wildcats had the ball. Cox fed Hatton with a beautiful pass in the lane, and he canned a short jumper to win it 61-60 while the Owls stood around in shock.

In the second semifinal, the high-flying Baylor took over after a tightly contested first half and scored 23 points with 22 rebounds. Seattle guard Charley Brown wowed the crowd with his dribbling skills, including a dazzling between-the-legs maneuver. The Chieftains won easily, 73-51.

Seattle was favored in the NCAA Final, but Kentucky was given a good chance because Baylor was nursing sore ribs. Hoping to wear Baylor down, Rupp told his players to make plenty of contact with the Chieftains' star. In the early stages of the game, Baylor seemed unaffected, and Seattle built up an 11-point bulge. By the end of the first half, however, Baylor was beginning to miss shots he normally made, and Kentucky cut the deficit to 3 points. In the second half, the aching Baylor could hardly buy a basket. Worse, he was whistled for his fourth foul—one more and he would be out of the game. To protect his star, coach John Castellani switched to a zone defense. Cox and Hatton came alive for the Wildcats, hitting for 35 points in the second half. Baylor could not respond, and Kentucky won 84-72.

> **Champion: Kentucky**
> **Winning Coach: Adolph Rupp**
> **Number of Schools in Tournament: 24**
> **Best Player: Elgin Baylor, Seattle**

1959
California Golden Bears
Cincinnati Bearcats
Louisville Cardinals
West Virginia Mountaineers

To win the 1959 NCAA Tournament, California coach Pete Newell needed to borrow from Phil Woolpert and Adolph Rupp. Like Woolpert and his back-to-back champions in San Francisco, Newell would need a total team defensive effort. Like Rupp, he would need to beat a pair of superstars with little in the way of top-flight talent. The Golden Bears had a good center named Darrall Imhoff and a dependable guard named Denny Fitzpatrick, but they hardly compared to Cincinnati's Oscar Robertson or West Virginia's Jerry West, the two most talked-about players in the country. Even the Louisville squad, which had upset Kentucky and Michigan State to reach the Final Four, seemed to have more pizzazz than California.

The 1958 title game was a rough one—just as Adolph Rupp had planned.

California coach Pete Newell had one of the best minds in basketball. His Golden Bears prevailed in an exciting championship game.

In the first semifinal, West Virginia pounded Louisville. The game was over after the first half during which West bombed the Cardinals from the perimeter and scored 38 points with 15 rebounds. The final score was 94-79. The second semifinal looked like it would be another wipeout, as Robertson tortured the Golden Bears with his passing, shooting, and spectacular drives to the basket. However, Newell's team managed to slow the pace down, and Robertson seemed to slow down with it. Cincinnati held a slim lead at the start of the second half, until California senior Al Buch hit several clutch shots to tie the score. The game turned when Robertson attempted a shot from the lane and Imhoff stuffed it back in his face. At the other end, Imhoff got the ball and canned a nifty hook shot to put the Golden Bears up by two. Robertson went right at Imhoff again, and again Imhoff rejected him. California held on for a 64-58 upset.

In the championship game, Newell suspected that West Virginia coach Fred Schaus would go for the jugular early. He told his players to press the Mountaineers right from the opening tip—if they wanted to score a lot of points early, they would have to expend a lot of energy doing so. Newell watched with concern as West helped his team build a 10-point lead. He felt better when the Mountaineers began making sloppy mistakes right before the half; as Newell had hoped, West Virginia was getting tired. California regained the lead before halftime but lost it in the second half when Schaus gave the Golden Bears a taste of their own medicine. Now it was West Virginia doing the pressing! With less than a minute left and the game hanging in the balance, Imhoff was called for goaltending when he batted away a shot by West. The center made up for this mistake, however, when he tipped in his own miss at the other end to give California a 3-point lead. West Virginia closed the gap to one point before the buzzer but fell 71-70.

Champion: California
Winning Coach: Pete Newell
Number of Schools in Tournament: 23
Best Player: Jerry West, West Virginia

THE 1960s

1960
California Golden Bears
Cincinnati Bearcats
NYU Violets
Ohio State Buckeyes

More so than in any previous year, the teams in the 1960 Final Four deserved to be there. With a combined record of 99-8, no school could be accused of "sneaking in." The California Golden Bears returned to defend their championship wiser and more confident, while Oscar Robertson's Cincinnati Bearcats looked practically unbeatable. NYU, which beat strong Duke and West Virginia teams to reach the Final Four, boasted one of the best all-around players in the tournament: Satch Sanders. Ohio State had a great junior in Larry Siegfried, along with a trio of hungry, energetic sophomores—Jerry Lucas, John Havlicek, and Mel Nowell—who seemed to get better with each game.

In the first semifinal, Ohio State mopped the floor with NYU. Sanders was helpless against Lucas and Havlicek, and his teammates seemed in awe of their surroundings for much of the afternoon. The Violets were never really in the game, which they lost 76-54.

On the other side of the draw, Cal and Cincinnati tangled in a rematch of the previous year's semifinal. This time, Robertson handled the tenacious defense better, and the Bearcats seemed in control for much of the first half. Then Cincinnati center Paul Hogue got into foul trouble, which allowed Darrall Imhoff to get the Golden Bears back in the contest. Robertson played brilliantly in the second half, but when Hogue fouled out, the game started slipping away. Imhoff and forward Bill McClintock went to work inside, and there was nothing Robertson or anyone else could do. California won 77-69.

The previous summer, Ohio State coach Fred Taylor had visited Newell to seek his advice—or as he put it, "to learn how to coach basketball." Taylor had run some interesting ideas by Newell, and the California coach had encouraged him to try them. Neither man could have dreamed that this meeting would lead to a rendezvous in the national championship game, but here they were. It was a classic battle between a great offensive team (the Buckeyes) and a great defensive team (the Golden Bears). Most fans picked California, whose players had more experience and more motivation—Newell had announced that this would be his last game as a college coach.

Oscar Robertson could shoot, pass, and dribble with either hand. He was the most complete player in the NCAA.

1961

Cincinnati Bearcats
St. Joseph's Hawks
Ohio State Buckeyes
Utah Utes

The graduation of Oscar Robertson was viewed by college basketball fans as a death blow to the Cincinnati program. Without the "Big O" in the lineup, no one expected much from the Bearcats—but here they were in the Final Four. Cincinnati was led by their new coach, Ed Jucker, who molded the team into a solid defensive unit and got the extra scoring he needed from Paul Hogue and Bob Wiesenhahn.

The other team from Ohio, Ohio State, was set to defend its 1960 NCAA title with the same strong group, led by Jerry Lucas, Larry Siegfried, and John Havlicek. Also in the mix were Utah, with former Kansas State coach Jack Gardner, and St. Joseph's, coached by Jack Ramsay. Ohio State was an enormous favorite, even after struggling in its first tournament game against Louisville.

The Buckeyes handled St. Joseph's with ease in the first semifinal. Lucas, Siegfried, and Havlicek missed only a total of five shots on the way to a 95-69 victory. In the other matchup, Cincinnati suffocated Utah in the first half and went into the locker room with a 35-20 lead. Senior guard Carl Bouldin lit it up from long range, while Hogue contributed 18 points and 14 rebounds. The Bearcats won, 82-67. It was their 21st victory in a row.

Yet as soon as the game began, it was clear that Ohio State had something extra. Lucas shut down Imhoff, and the team hit 16 of 19 field goal attempts in the first half. Meanwhile, Ohio State's defense was smothering; at halftime, California still had not reached 20 points. It looked like the Bearcats were mounting a comeback early in the second half, but the Buckeyes continued to hit more than half of their shots. The final score was 75-55. Afterward, a gracious Taylor credited his team's amazing performance to the guidance of his California counterpart a year earlier. For Newell, it was a touching sentiment, but little consolation for a humiliating loss.

SCANDALS OF '61

In the weeks following the 1961 Final Four, an investigation turned up evidence that players at 22 schools were involved in—or had knowledge of—a point-shaving scheme masterminded by New York gamblers. It worked the same way it had a decade earlier. Players on teams favored to win by big margins made sure to shoot and pass poorly enough so that their teams only won by a few points. Sometimes they overdid it, and the result was a loss. The gamblers would wager heavily on the underdog, and then collect their winnings when the favorites failed to "cover the spread." The players—all desperate for cash—were paid a few hundred dollars each for their part in the plan.

As it spread from New York to schools all over the country the investigation made headlines nationwide. In their zeal to uncover the widening conspiracy, detectives often decided that players were guilty before learning all the facts. When they could not prove any wrongdoing, they sometimes tried to cover themselves by getting players to admit they had talked to some of the gamblers. When this testimony was turned over to a player's school, he was immediately kicked out for not reporting the conversation—even when no discussions of point-shaving had taken place. Colleges were so intent on getting rid of their bad apples that they got rid of a few good ones in the process. It was a classic case of guilt by association.

One such player was Connie Hawkins, a Brooklyn high-school star who had accepted a scholarship to Iowa. All he had done was to casually talk to one of the fixers, and they had never even discussed the plot. When the naïve teenager was questioned by police months later, the officers forced a "confession," and Hawkins was banned from college ball. Those who saw him play in the early 1960s claim "Hawk" was the best player alive. And in playground contests against NBA stars such as Wilt Chamberlain, Hawkins did indeed dominate. Although the NBA was aware of how thin the evidence was against Hawkins, the league banned him anyway. Left to showcase his talents in the backwaters of basketball, Hawkins wasted his best years playing for the Harlem Globetrotters, Pittsburgh Rens, and Minnesota Pipers. He eventually sued the NBA and won the right to play, but knee injuries had reduced him to a shadow of his former greatness.

Many of the players who were accused of shaving points were actually guilty. Jack Egan, who led St. Joseph's to the Final Four in 1961, admitted to taking money. As the team's star, Egan typically took 20 or more shots a game. Who would notice if he happened to miss a few in a game that the Hawks won anyway?

This statistic meant little to the experts, who still predicted that Ohio State would overwhelm Cincinnati in the final. They began to change their minds, however, when they saw how tough Hogue played Lucas. He bumped and banged and pushed the All-American down the court every time. Finally Lucas began to shoot from outside. Although he made his shots and Ohio State grabbed the lead, Hogue had succeeded in taking Fred Taylor's Buckeyes out of their game plan. Bouldin was hot again, and he kept the Bearcats close. At intermission, Ohio State had a mere one-point lead.

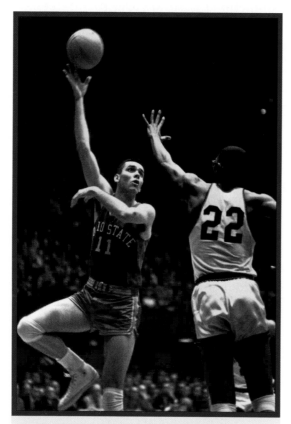

Jerry Lucas flips a hook shot over Paul Hogue. Hogue's aggressive defense proved the difference in the 1961 NCAA final.

The contest became even more physical in the second half, and Cincinnati took a 2-point lead with time running out. Reserve guard Bobby Knight got the Buckeyes even with a clutch layup, and the championship went into overtime. Lucas fouled Hogue at the beginning of the 5-minute period, and the Cincinnati center, normally erratic from the line, surprised everyone by hitting two free throws. From there, the Bearcats' defense clamped down and held the lead, winning 70-65.

> **Champion: Cincinnati**
> **Winning Coach: Ed Jucker**
> **Number of Schools in Tournament: 24**
> **Best Player: Jerry Lucas, Ohio State**

1962
Cincinnati Bearcats
Ohio State Buckeyes
UCLA Bruins
Wake Forest Demon Deacons

The 1961–62 season was a tough one for the Cincinnati Bearcats. Their win over Ohio State in the 1961 NCAA Final was considered a fluke, and they watched in dismay as Jerry Lucas grabbed all the headlines by winning Player of the Year honors. Ed Jucker's team entered the NCAA Tournament looking for respect. When the Final Four field was set, the Bearcats knew they would have their chance. Wake Forest had a couple of dynamite shooters in Billy Packer and Len Chappell, along with a smart coach in Bones McKinney. UCLA, under coach John Wooden, was a dangerous squad. Like Wooden in his playing days, the Bruins were in great condition and had perfect fun-

damentals. And, of course, there were the Buckeyes—looming on the horizon, waiting for their chance to avenge their loss a year earlier. Whoever won the championship this year was really going to earn it.

In the first semifinal, Havlicek played Chappell to a draw and Lucas dominated inside to give the Buckeyes an insurmountable second-half lead. With 6 minutes left and the game in hand, Lucas limped off the court after landing awkwardly on his knee. Although Ohio State still won easily, there was little postgame celebrating in the locker room.

In the second game, Cincinnati opened up a 14-point lead but could not finish off UCLA. Led by John Green, the Bruins clawed back to tie the score at halftime, 37-37. The second half was an interesting battle between Cincinnati's two frontcourt stars, Paul Hogue and Ron Bonham, and

UCLA's backcourt, which featured Green and Walt Hazzard. Scoring 14 consecutive points, Hogue was a one-man gang down the stretch. With 10 seconds left, the game was deadlocked at 70-70. The Bruins, expecting the ball to go to Hogue, crowded around the Cincinnati center. Junior guard Tom Thacker—who had missed all 6 of his shots—fired up a 25-footer, and it found the bottom of the net for a buzzer-beating victory.

Suddenly Cincinnati—not Ohio State—was looking like the team to beat. With their confidence high and the dreaded Lucas at less than 100 percent, the Bearcats had the Buckeyes right where they wanted them. Once Jucker saw how easily Hogue was out-rebounding Lucas, he instructed Bonham to move outside when the team had the ball. This forced Havlicek, the man defending him, to move out, too. Without "Hondo" to help him on the boards, Lucas was unable to trigger the fast break, and the game turned into a slow, defensive battle—Cincinnati's specialty. The Bearcats got great games from Hogue and the superconfident Thacker and went on to win 71-59. Jucker and his players now had back-to-back NCAA championships, along with enough respect to last a lifetime.

Champion: Cincinnati
Winning Coach: Ed Jucker
Number of Schools in Tournament: 25
Best Player: Paul Hogue, Cincinnati

1963
Cincinnati Bearcats
Duke Blue Devils
Loyola-Chicago Ramblers
Oregon State Beavers

Although African-Americans had played key roles in many Final Fours, it was not until Cincinnati won back-to-back championships that fans began to take notice of what they brought to the college game. The Bearcats were quick, tough, aggressive, and smart. They beat opponents to loose balls and outmuscled them for rebounds. In other words, they won. And because this team did not have a Bill Russell or an Oscar Robertson or an Elgin Baylor, they won with spectacular team play—something that many white coaches mistakenly insisted black players could not do.

Cincinnati returned to the Final Four in 1963, but it was the Loyola team from Chicago that was the talk of the tournament. The Ramblers had four black starters—Jerry Harkness, Les Hunter, Vic Rouse, and Ron Miller—along with Johnny Egan, a white forward. It was a "first" in Final Four competition. Duke and Oregon State were the other two teams. The Blue Devils were led by All-American guards Art Heyman and Jeff Mullins. The Beavers looked to Mel Counts, a mobile 7-footer, who was the best center in the tournament.

The Ramblers, losers of just two games all year, played a fast-paced style that often left opponents gasping for air. The team's go-to guy was Harkness, a wizard from the playgrounds of New York City. In the first semifinal Harkness was cold, but Hunter and Miller picked up the slack. Loyola built a solid lead, but late in the second half Duke came storming back to within three points. The Blue Devils stalled, however, and Loyola pulled away, 94-75. Cincinnati's game against Oregon State was a blowout. Counts dictated play early but ran into foul trouble against the Bearcats. With their big man on the bench, the Beavers watched in disappointment as Cincinnati won 80-46.

For Cincinnati to win three NCAA titles in a row, the Bearcats had to lure Loyola into a rugged half-court game. Ed Jucker's players pressured the ball all the way up the court, then settled into a tricky man-to-man defense. The strategy worked, and the Ramblers looked uncomfortable for most of the game. Six minutes into the second half, the Bearcats had a commanding 14-point lead. Jucker commanded them to stall. Loyola started playing desperate, high-energy defense, and suddenly the momentum shifted. Meanwhile, Tom Thacker, George Wilson, and Tony Yates all got into foul trouble for Cincinnati. Loyola kept pouring it on until they found themselves trailing by just two, 54-52. With 4 seconds left, Harkness made

Ron Miller, Johnny Egan, and Jerry Harkness flank Loyola coach George Ireland.

the game-tying shot to send the contest into overtime.

In the 5-minute OT, Harkness again had the ball in his hands at the key moment— with the game tied and just a few seconds left. This time he drove to the hoop but found Ron Bonham in his path. Harkness whipped the ball back to Hunter, who let fly from the foul circle. His shot went off the rim, but Rouse swooped in and tipped it into the basket to give Loyola the championship. The Ramblers' 60-58 win still ranks among the most thrilling in Final Four history.

> **Champion: Loyola-Chicago**
> **Winning Coach: George Ireland**
> **Number of Schools in Tournament: 25**
> **Best Player: Art Heyman, Duke**

1964
Duke Blue Devils
Kansas State Wildcats
Michigan Wolverines
UCLA Bruins

Building a college basketball "dynasty" is no easy task. It took John Wooden eight years to win his first NCAA Tournament game and six more before his Bruins reached the Final Four in 1962. In 1964, UCLA put it all together and achieved an undefeated season. Wooden had finally found the right mix of discipline, conditioning, and talent. Senior Walt Hazzard was joined in the backcourt by Gail Goodrich, a fearless and determined offensive player who demanded a double-team whenever he touched the ball. Their supporting cast was made up of role players like Keith Erickson, Ken Washington, and Fred Slaughter. These were excellent athletes who agreed to fit into Wooden's system; when Goodrich or Hazzard went cold, they were capable of stepping up and taking charge.

The other teams in the Final Four were Duke, Kansas State, and Michigan. With Art Heyman graduated, the Blue Devils were now Jeff Mullins' team, and with Vic Bubas calling the shots from the sideline, they were an offensive powerhouse. Kansas State, coached by Tex Winter, featured Willie Murrell. The Wolverines of Michigan had the best chance of taking down UCLA. A sparkling defense led by Oliver Darden and Bill Buntin was balanced by the scoring exploits of forward Cazzie Russell.

Duke and Michigan squared off in the first semifinal, and the Blue Devils simply overpowered the Wolverines. The defense did its job against Mullins and forward Jack Marin but could not control Duke's re-

Walt Hazzard turns the corner for UCLA. He led a comeback with 8 minutes left in the NCAA semifinal.

Bruins poured it on in one of their famous "2-minute explosions." Hazzard ignited the fast break, and before Winter knew what hit him, the game was as good as over. UCLA won 90-84.

The championship showdown pitted UCLA's speed against Duke's size. Each team had senior leadership and talented underclassmen. Wooden was a better coach than Vic Bubas, but each man knew he was in for a struggle. Duke drew first blood with several shots from the paint. Then the Bruins found their rhythm midway through the first half and transformed a 3-point deficit into a 12-point halftime lead. In the second half, both teams shot well, and Duke could not make up the difference. The game was never really in jeopardy for UCLA, which won 98-83.

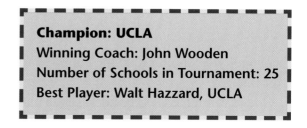

Champion: UCLA
Winning Coach: John Wooden
Number of Schools in Tournament: 25
Best Player: Walt Hazzard, UCLA

1965
Michigan Wolverines
Princeton Tigers
UCLA Bruins
Wichita State Shockers

Basketball fans could not have asked for a more interesting group of teams than the 1965 Final Four. There was UCLA, defending its championship with All-American Gail Goodrich, Keith Erickson, Ken Washington, and Edgar Lacey. There was Michigan, better and stronger than the year before, with Cazzie Russell having a sensational year. Princeton, with sharpshooting

bounding and inside scoring. The Blue Devils opened up a 9-point lead at halftime and cruised to a 91-80 victory.

Kansas State did a much better job against UCLA. The Wildcats forced the action and got the Bruins into foul trouble. Matching UCLA shot-for-shot, they grabbed a 5-point lead with less than 8 minutes left in the game. Wooden's players had been in this situation before, so they did not panic. When Kansas State let up just slightly, the

Bill Bradley, gave Ivy Leaguers a team to root for. Wichita State beat the odds and made it to the Final Four despite the fact that super-scorer Dave Stallworth and 7-footer Nate Bowman were ruled ineligible for tournament play.

In a replay of the season's most compelling game, Russell and Bradley faced off in the first semifinal. Michigan and Princeton had waged an epic battle in December 1964, with the top-ranked Wolverines squeaking out a narrow victory. Michigan went right after Bradley in this game. Although he scored 29 points, the senior forward had three fouls at halftime and fouled

Bill Bradley takes the ball to the hoop against Michigan in the national semifinal. Bradley's Princeton Tigers lost, but he was named the tournament's top player.

out in the second half. Russell and Bill Buntin had big games and led the Wolverines to a 93-76 victory.

UCLA had even less trouble with Wichita State. The Bruins ran the Shockers out of the building, outscoring their opponents 65-38 in the first half. They eased up in the second half but still won 108-89.

Although they were defending champions, the UCLA Bruins were actually underdogs in the NCAA Final. Michigan, it seemed, was just too strong defensively and a much better rebounding team. Wooden's best hope for a repeat was to wear down the slower Wolverines, then unleash Goodrich on them. The plan looked good on paper but bad on the court—Michigan not only kept up with the Bruins, but also established a 20-13 lead.

Then something magical happened. As Wooden expected, the Wolverines began huffing and puffing. Meanwhile, Goodrich put on a show. He did not simply score baskets; he dribbled around and through the defense, engaging all five opponents on some plays, which tired them out even more. UCLA surged into the lead, and by the second half the Bruins were ahead by 20. By this time, all the Michigan players could do was flail at Goodrich, and their three best defenders—Buntin, Oliver Darden, and Larry Tregoning—fouled out. In all, Goodrich went to the foul line 20 times and made 18 free throws. He finished the game with 42 points, and UCLA won 91-80.

Champion: UCLA
Winning Coach: John Wooden
Number of Schools in Tournament: 23
Best Player: Bill Bradley, Princeton

1966

Duke Blue Devils
Kentucky Wildcats
Texas Western Miners
Utah Utes

The impact of African-American players on college basketball had become clear by the mid-1960s. The vertical style that emerged from city playgrounds was changing the sport in important ways. Brawny, earthbound defenders were no longer able to deal with the explosion of fluid drivers and jump-shooters in the college game, and it showed in the high scoring averages around the country. The quickness and leaping ability of these players gave coaches a talent pool from which they could instantly upgrade their defenses. More and more college scholarships found their way into the inner cities.

When Don Haskins was hired to coach tiny Texas Western in the border town of El Paso, he knew just where to recruit a team. In 1965–1966, the Miners' seven best players were African-American. They were led by Bobby Joe Hill, a 5-foot-9 guard from New York City. The team's key frontcourt players were David "Big Daddy D" Lattin and Nevil "Shadow" Shed. They were not superstars, but they were hungry and smart and ready to make some history.

The other teams in the Final Four were Utah, Duke, and Kentucky. Jack Gardner's Utes were led by Jerry Chambers, a do-it-all forward capable of scoring 40 points a game. Duke featured Jack Marin and Bob Verga, who often combined for 40 to 50 a night. Kentucky, with Adolph Rupp still at the helm and stars Louie Dampier and Pat Riley, was the tournament favorite. The old man still believed that an all-white team

Bobby Joe Hill streaks past a Kentucky defender in the 1966 NCAA Final. Texas Western shocked the Wildcats and opened the eyes of basketball coaches around the country.

was the best way to go for the Wildcats. He and a few other southern coaches refused to recruit black players. As Kentucky and Texas Western moved closer and closer to a showdown, the basketball world watched with great interest.

The first semifinal saw Kentucky and Duke play in what many considered to be the "real" college championship; both squads seemed far superior to either Utah or Texas Western. Although Verga was fighting the flu, Duke gave the Wildcats a good game. The Blue Devils battled Rupp's tight zone by hitting long jumpers and went into intermission ahead by one point. Kentucky switched to man-to-man in the second half, but Duke continued to play tough. The game finally turned on a loose ball. Kentucky's Larry Conley grabbed it and barreled in for a layup to give the Wildcats a four-point lead, and they held on to win a tense game, 83-79.

In the second semifinal, Coach Haskins watched as Chambers riddled his defense for 38 points. Whenever a Miner touched the Utah star, the refs whistled him for a foul. It was a frustrating experience, but Texas Western won the game 85-78 thanks to the clutch shooting of Orsten Artis.

Kentucky was given a huge edge in the championship game. To the naked eye, the Wildcats were every bit as fast as the Miners and were superior shooters, rebounders, and defenders. What the naked eye did not see, however, was that the Texas Western players were a split second quicker to the ball, and this would throw the Wildcats ever so slightly off their game. This was not clear at first. Kentucky bunched up in a zone and challenged Texas Western to shoot from the outside. When they did not make their shots, the Wildcats took the lead. As the first half wore on, however, the Miners began making plays, and they went into the locker room with a 34-31 advantage.

Haskins told his players to turn up the defensive heat in the second half, and this resulted in a slew of steals and intercepted passes. When Kentucky did get a good look at the basket, often the shots fell short—a clear sign of fatigue. Although the Wildcats stayed within striking range, they never closed the gap. Texas Western, an unknown all-black team, had defeated the most famous all-white team in the land, 72-65. Within months, schools like Davidson and North Carolina began recruiting African-

Americans. Even Rupp grudgingly changed his views. In fact, it was a black player who delivered Kentucky's next NCAA title.

> **Champion: Texas Western**
> **Winning Coach: Don Haskins**
> **Number of Schools in Tournament: 22**
> **Best Player: Jerry Chambers, Utah**

1967
Dayton Flyers
Houston Cougars
North Carolina Tar Heels
UCLA Bruins

When the final buzzer sounded on UCLA's 1965 championship, few fans realized just how much they had to celebrate. John Wooden's back-to-back NCAA titles helped him recruit a 7-foot-2 center from New York City who had the moves of a forward and the mind of a professor. His name was Lew Alcindor, and he would be the key to continuing Wooden's basketball dynasty. Because freshmen were not allowed to compete in varsity sports during the 1960s, Alcindor had to play for the Bruins' junior varsity team in 1965–66. The varsity squad struggled to an 18-8 record and did not receive an NCAA Tournament bid. Writers that year joked that the best team in the country was the UCLA JV, and the truth is that they might have been right. With Alcindor in the middle, the JV usually beat the varsity in team scrimmages!

One season later, the UCLA varsity went undefeated, and Alcindor averaged 29 points and 15.5 rebounds per game. The "Big Lew" had a great supporting cast. Wooden had recruited two superb guards in Lucius Allen

Lew Alcindor wheels to the basket against Dayton. The UCLA center scored 20 points and grabbed 18 rebounds in the championship game.

tried desperately to make a game of it in the second half, but every Cougar miss seemed to turn into a Bruin fast break. Alcindor was the key on both ends. He grabbed 20 rebounds and made Hayes miss 19 shots, while his crisp passes prevented the Cougars from double- and triple-teaming him.

Dayton's only hope in the NCAA final was UCLA's lack of experience. Wooden's young recruits had never been to the Big Dance. In fact, there was not a single senior on the team. The crowd got excited when the Flyers played the Bruins even for a few minutes, but Alcindor shut down the middle and forced May and company to shoot from outside. When Dayton's shots stopped dropping, UCLA began to pull away. A 38-20 halftime lead soon approached 30 points. In the final minutes, Wooden benched his starters and let his substitutes play. Dayton scored some late baskets to make the score respectable, but the game was never really close. The final was 79-64.

and Mike Warren, while Lynn Shackelford and Ken Heitz flanked Alcindor on the front line. The only team with a chance to beat the Bruins was Houston, which had whirlwind center Elvin Hayes and defensive specialist Don Chaney at guard. Neither Dayton, led by Don May, nor UNC, led by Larry Miller, had a realistic chance of winning it all.

Still, one of these teams would reach the final, because Houston and UCLA were both in the western bracket. Don Donoher's Flyers trounced Dean Smith's Tar Heels, 76-62. May scored 34 points and 15 rebounds. The other semifinal was close for about 10 minutes. Houston was holding its own until Wooden decided to apply a full-court press. The Bruins smothered the Cougars, as Allen and Shackelford keyed an 11-0 run. Houston

Champion: UCLA
Winning Coach: John Wooden
Number of Schools in Tournament: 23
Best Player: Lew Alcindor, UCLA

1968
Houston Cougars
North Carolina Tar Heels
Ohio State Buckeyes
UCLA Bruins

John Wooden had one heck of a team. Coming off a national championship season, he had kept all of his starters and improved his bench. UCLA's only loss during the season came at the hands of the Houston Cougars, and it ended a 47-game winning streak. The game had been held in the Astrodome before the largest crowd in the history of college basketball. Fans of the Bruins dismissed the loss, pointing out that Lew Alcindor had played with a scratched eye. Nevertheless, Elvin Hayes and the Cougars had accomplished the "impossible."

If a team could beat the Bruins once, it could happen again. Everyone, including Wooden, was aware of this fact. For obvious reasons, Houston was best suited to do it. But the Tar Heels were no pushovers, either. Larry Miller was back, along with Charlie Scott, the school's first great African-American star. Rounding out the Final Four was Ohio State, rebuilt by Fred Taylor with stars Bill Hoskett and Steve Howell.

Once again, the tournament's marquee game took place in the semifinals. Guy Lewis's Cougars wanted to put their stamp on a super season, while the Bruins were looking for revenge. Houston was on a roll, with big victories over Loyola, Louisville, and Texas Christian. Hayes had scored 49, 35, and 39 in the three games and had averaged 25 rebounds per contest. Wooden decided to have forward Lynn Shackelford "shadow" Hayes, guarding him closely the instant Houston took possession of the ball. This freed up Alcindor to clog the middle, and to double-team Hayes whenever he came inside. The poor Houston center hardly touched the ball during the first half. After about 10 minutes, the Bruins began to take control, and by halftime, they were up by 22 points. In the second half, the humiliation continued. UCLA kept pouring it on and at one stage had a 44-point lead. The final score was 101-69.

On the other side of the bracket, Dean Smith guided his troops to victory with a

UCLA's blowout of Houston in the semifinals was bigger news than its victory over UNC in the title game. Lew Alcindor outscored Elvin Hayes 19–10.

strong defensive effort. The starting five for the Buckeyes shot a miserable 18-for-59 from the field and lost the game 80-66.

The final was not as lopsided as the Houston game, but the Bruins were in control from start to finish. Alcindor let the Tar Heels know who was boss by blocking half a dozen shots in the first few minutes. Mike Warren and Lucius Allen also played great defense. A 10-point halftime lead grew to more than 20 in the second half, as Alcindor rained "sky hooks" down on the helpless Tar Heel defenders. When the buzzer sounded, the big man had 34 points and 16 rebounds in an easy 78-55 win.

I AM THIRD

From 1946 to 1981, the losing teams in the first Final Four games went on to play each other in a game held prior to the national championship. This was called the National Third Place game, and it featured some wild contests over the years. The two losing teams often forgot about defense and just tried to outscore each other. Because the stats from these games were counted in the official tournament records, many of the greatest performances in Final Four history were produced in these meaningless free-for-alls. That is one of the reasons the game was eventually abolished.

If you want to stump an expert with a trivia question, ask which school won the most National Third Place games. The answer is Illinois, which took the NCAA's consolation prize three times between 1949 and 1952. The two highest-scoring players in a Final Four game set their records in National Third Place games: Bill Bradley scored 58 for Princeton in 1965, and Temple's Hal Lear poured in 48 in 1956. The three highest team scores in Final Four history are 127, 120, and 118—all in National Third Place games. Perhaps the most curious legacy of these games is that four of the NCAA's Most Outstanding Player awards (Bradley, Lear, Utah's Jerry Chambers, and Duke's Art Heyman) went to players whose final game of the year occurred in the consolation match instead of the NCAA Final!

Champion: UCLA
Winning Coach: John Wooden
Number of Schools in Tournament: 23
Best Player: Lew Alcindor, UCLA

1969
Drake Bulldogs
North Carolina Tar Heels
Purdue Boilermakers
UCLA Bruins

Was Lew Alcindor the key to UCLA's dominance? Or had it been the play of John Wooden's great guards? The Bruins answered these question by losing just one game during the 1968–1969 season, despite the graduation of Lucius Allen and Mike Warren. John Vallely proved a capable replacement at guard, while forwards Curtis Rowe and Sidney Wicks blended beautifully with Lynn Shackelford on the front line. Still, the lack of superstar guards left a little opening for UCLA's Final Four foes, each of whom had a big-time backcourt star.

Purdue's Rick Mount was a shot-making machine who regularly poured in 30 to 40 points a night. His backcourt mate, Billy Keller, was also a superb player. Drake's Willie McCarter was one of the most dangerous guards in the tournament;

High-scoring Rick Mount, who was shut down in the 1969 NCAA Final. Ken Heitz of the Bruins limited him to just 12-of-36 from the field.

when teams doubled up on him, that freed up Willie Wise, a forward with a lethal inside game. And then there was UNC's Charlie Scott, fresh off the U.S. Olympic team, who was a solid 20-point scorer for Dean Smith's Tar Heels.

UCLA's first Final Four opponent was Drake. The Willies both played marvelously, as McCarter hit from all over the court and Wise battled Alcindor for every rebound. At halftime, the Bulldogs trailed by just a single basket. With 5 minutes left in the second half, Drake actually took the lead. Yet as so often happened against the Bruins, their marvelous center took control of the game. On three straight possessions, Drake players penetrated to the hoop only to have Alcindor slap their shots away. Vallely, who played well all game, made the Bulldogs pay with clutch baskets on the

other end, and suddenly UCLA was up by a dozen points. Undaunted, Drake came storming back and pulled to within one point with 7 seconds left. The Bulldogs fouled Shackelford intentionally, hoping he would miss his free throws. But the senior drained both shots, and UCLA advanced to the championship game, 85-82.

Purdue had an easier time with North Carolina. Mount and Keller ganged up on Scott, limiting him to 16 points. The Boilermakers pulled away in the second half and won 92-65. Their two stars combined for 56 points.

After surviving the scare against Drake, the Bruins knew they needed to be focused against Purdue. UCLA came out sharp in the opening minutes of the final, with Alcindor hitting several shots. Meanwhile, senior Ken Heitz shadowed Mount, just as Shackelford had Elvin Hayes a year before. The desperate Mount missed 24 shots. Worse, the players charged with guarding Alcindor fouled out early in the second half, and he began scoring points in bunches. After the big guy recorded his 37th point, even Wooden could not bear to watch him beat up on the Boilermaker reserves and took him out. UCLA glided to a 92-72 victory. Although the postgame celebrating was spirited, one could not help but wonder whether this great dynasty was finally at an end. With Alcindor due to graduate and no superstar waiting to replace him, it looked like it might be a while before the Bruins returned to the Final Four.

Champion: UCLA
Winning Coach: John Wooden
Number of Schools in Tournament: 25
Best Player: Lew Alcindor, UCLA

CHAPTER 4

THE 1970s

1970

Jacksonville Dolphins
New Mexico State Aggies
St. Bonaventure Bonnies
UCLA Bruins

Despite its lack of a top-notch big man, UCLA still made it back to the Final Four. The play of Curtis Rowe, Sidney Wicks, and point guard Henry Bibby made up for the so-so skills of 6-foot-9 Steve Patterson, the Bruins' new center. For UCLA to win its fourth consecutive championship, however, Patterson would have to come up big. Both of the teams the Bruins were likely to meet in the Final Four had dominant pivot men. New Mexico State's Sam Lacey was a solid offensive player who worked well with forward Jimmy Collins and guard Charlie Criss. And Jacksonville's 7-2 Artis Gilmore was the scariest player in the country. St. Bonaventure probably had the best all-around center in the tournament, Bob Lanier, but he had injured his knee in the East Regional final against Villanova and was unable to play.

In the first semifinal, St. Bonaventure really pulled together and gave Jacksonville a good game. They outhustled the Dolphins and kept the contest close right

Curtis Rowe of UCLA launches a jumper over the outstretched arm of Artis Gilmore. Rowe led the Bruins with 19 points in the championship game.

until the final minutes, when the Bonnies simply ran out of gas. UCLA had an easier game against New Mexico State. John Wooden employed a full-court press for much of the game, which put the pressure on Criss and Collins and kept the ball out of Lacey's hands. Collins responded with a marvelous shooting performance, but Lacey made only three of nine shots. With all five Bruin starters playing well, UCLA had no trouble rolling to a 93-77 victory.

The championship game began with Wicks—not Patterson—bumping and elbowing with Gilmore. The Jacksonville giant proved too much for one man, however, and soon UCLA found itself trailing by 9 points. Wooden commanded Patterson to help Wicks, and between the two of them they managed to deny Gilmore the ball. Toward the end of the first half, the Bruins went on a 9-0 run and regained the lead. In the second half, Gilmore was exhausted from UCLA's double-team. Wicks, on the other hand, seemed energized by it. He would wait for Gilmore to make his move on Patterson and either swat his shot away or force him to change it. Wicks even outrebounded Gilmore.

Inspired by this turn of events, the Bruins clamped down on the rest of the Dolphins and held them to a mere 69 points—33 below their average for the tournament. When the buzzer sounded, UCLA was national champion again, 80-69. As for Patterson, his numbers glowed next to Gilmore's. Although Wooden had recruited a big redhead named Bill Walton to step into the middle, Patterson would have to keep the position warm for one more season.

Champion: UCLA
Winning Coach: John Wooden
Number of Schools in Tournament: 25
Best Player: Sidney Wicks, UCLA

1971
Kansas Jayhawks
UCLA Bruins
Villanova Wildcats
Western Kentucky Hilltoppers

By the time UCLA reached the 1971 Final Four, the team's front line was functioning like a well-oiled machine. Curtis Rowe, Sidney Wicks, and Steve Patterson each did his share of dirty work under the basket, and they played together as well as any threesome in college basketball. The Bruins' guards, Henry Bibby and Terry Schoefield, were good ball handlers and excellent defenders. On paper, this team looked good, but not great. On the hardwood, however, its record was a spectacular 29-1.

That is why experts gave Kansas, Villanova, and Western Kentucky little chance of unseating UCLA as national champion. Not that these schools lacked the talent to win—on the contrary, each had at least one player who probably could have started for John Wooden. Western Kentucky's Jim McDaniels was one of the best centers in the country, while Bud Stallworth and Dave Robisch gave Kansas a formidable front line. Howard Porter of Villanova was one of the most dynamic forwards to come along in years.

The Wildcats and the Hilltoppers waged an epic battle in their Final Four matchup. Porter was a one-man wrecking crew for Villanova. He scored 22 points, grabbed 16

A QUESTION OF CLASS

As long as there has been college basketball, a controversy has raged over which players should be playing and which should not. The first big debate of the modern era came during World War II (1939–45), when tens of thousands of older students left school and joined the military. With many universities struggling just to fill the uniforms they owned, the NCAA relaxed its long-standing rule forbidding freshmen to play at the varsity level.

During the 1950s, when individual stars began to dominate the college game, many fans and coaches wondered why a freshman who would likely be the best player on the varsity had no choice but to play on the junior varsity for a year. A few also wondered why players could not leave college early and turn professional. The answer was that the NBA did not want to upset the NCAA, which was acting like a free "minor league." Pro basketball was not the big-money sport it is now; the NCAA was far more powerful. When Wilt Chamberlain left Kansas prior to his senior season, he had to barnstorm with the Harlem Globetrotters before the NBA would take him.

In the 1960s, the same debates raged, but this time with a new wrinkle. As African-Americans began to play a more important role in college basketball, this understanding between the NCAA and the NBA came under greater scrutiny. Colleges were now recruiting heavily in America's inner cities, offering poor teenagers an education in return for their basketball talents. Many of these players became major stars, and by their junior or senior years they were clearly good enough to make it as professionals. But because the NBA had agreed not to draft a player before his senior class graduated, these players—whose families were sometimes living in squalor while they guiltily lived it up on campus—were put in unfair situations. Soon a handful of top college players, claiming "hardship," got around the regulations and left school early.

The newly formed American Basketball Association, desperate for talent, played a key role in this process. The ABA had no such rule about signing underclassmen.

rebounds, and played furious defense. The 7-foot-1 McDaniels also scored 22 and pulled down 17 rebounds. The game itself was as close as the statistics of these two stars. Villanova led 39-36 at the half, but Western Kentucky kept within a few points and tied the game at the end of regulation. Hilltoppers guard Jerry Dunn actually had a chance to win the game but missed a pair of free throws with 4 seconds left. Each school scored 11 points in overtime, forcing a second 5 minute period. With McDaniels and Dunn fouled out, Porter took over and boosted Villanova into the final with a 92-89 win.

The UCLA-Kansas game was less hectic but also exciting. The Bruins carved out

In 1969, the Denver Rockets grabbed sophomore Spencer Haywood, who had led the NCAA in rebounding with the University of Detroit. People who claimed that juniors and seniors would be overwhelmed in the pros watched as Haywood won the ABA's Most Valuable Player award. Haywood then set his sights on the NBA and signed a lucrative deal with the Seattle Supersonics. The other NBA teams told the Sonics to forget it—Haywood still had another year of college eligibility, and they were not changing the rule. When Seattle's owner threatened to sue the NBA, the league relented. This decision led to a loophole that allowed an impoverished player to leave school early and auction his services between the NBA and the ABA.

Through this loophole flowed some of the college game's best talent. It is hard to say whether this had a direct effect on the Final Four, because there was no guarantee that the players who left early would have advanced that far. What happened next had a tremendous impact on the tournament however. To make up for the players being siphoned off by the pros, the NCAA finally decided to let freshmen play varsity ball, starting in the 1972–1973 season.

In the old days, many of the programs that returned to the championship round again and again did so because they stockpiled freshman talent on their junior varsity teams. In the 1950s and 1960s, high-school stars were lured to these schools with the promise that, if they waited a couple of years, they too could play in the Final Four. With freshmen eligible, these programs now had to compete with smaller schools, who could promise high-school seniors that they would start right away. The immediate result was that the country's basketball talent started to spread out. Coaches who were always one player short of a great team could now get that player. So instead of a couple of great teams and a bunch of good ones, the NCAA Tournament now had a dozen or more very good teams every year. In 1975, the level of play was high enough to increase the tournament field to 48 schools; in 1985, the field reached 64.

a 7-point halftime lead, then turned back repeated challenges in the second half with clutch shots by Bibby, Rowe, and Wicks. The final score was 68-60, UCLA.

What scared UCLA about Villanova was not Porter, but coach Jack Kraft's stellar zone defense. In order to win his fifth championship in a row, Wooden believed he had to force the Wildcats to play man-to-man. The best way to do this was to establish a lead and then "stall"—a strategy that was unfamiliar to the Bruins. By halftime, UCLA had the lead it was looking for, and on Wooden's orders his players slowed the game down to a crawl. Boos and jeers echoed throughout the cavernous Astrodome as the Bruins worked the ball around the perimeter and only took shots they were certain they could make.

Although the Wildcats cut the lead to 3 points, they never got any closer, and UCLA won 68-62. The much-maligned Patterson, in his last college game, gave the performance of a lifetime. He hit 13 of 18 shots and finished with 29 points. Wicks, also playing for the last time in a UCLA uniform, was criticized for only scoring 7 points. But, as usual, the senior had made a difference in ways that do not show up in the box score. As far as Coach Wooden was concerned, Sidney had never played better.

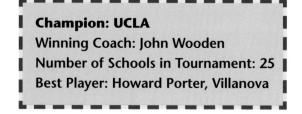

Champion: UCLA
Winning Coach: John Wooden
Number of Schools in Tournament: 25
Best Player: Howard Porter, Villanova

1972
Florida State Seminoles
Louisville Cardinals
North Carolina Tar Heels
UCLA Bruins

College basketball had its chance to dethrone UCLA in 1970 and 1971, when John

John Wooden holds the NCAA championship trophy for the seventh time in eight seasons.

Wooden was without a true center. Now it was too late. A 6-foot-11 sophomore named Bill Walton was on the squad, as was 6-foot-6 Keith Wilkes. Both were big upgrades over the seniors they replaced, and the Bruins still had Henry Bibby to run the offense. Walton seemed born to play in the UCLA system. He began his basketball life as a guard, so he could shoot, dribble, and pass. This made him almost impossible to guard one-on-one, and also difficult to double-team. The instant Walton saw a second defender coming, he would whip a pass to the teammate who had just been left unguarded. On defense, Walton could move quickly from side to side and jump higher than other centers, and he was big enough to outmuscle anyone who challenged him inside. So it came as no surprise when the Bruins—who were undefeated entering the 1972 NCAA Tournament— reached the Final Four by obliterating good teams from Weber State and Long Beach State.

UCLA's first victim, Louisville, relied on the scoring of guard Jimmy Price and the dynamic coaching talent of young Denny Crum, who had learned his craft as an assistant to Wooden in the 1960s. On the other side of the draw waited power forward Bob McAdoo of the Tar Heels and guard Ron King of the Seminoles. If anyone in the tournament was capable of handling Walton, it was the 6-foot-9 McAdoo. He was the best-shooting big man to come along in years.

McAdoo played well against Florida State in the first semifinal, but there was nothing he could do about Otto Petty. The 5-foot-7 floor leader of the Seminoles squirted through Dean Smith's defense time and again. At halftime, the Tar Heels found themselves down by 13 points. They staged a great comeback in the second half but fell short when McAdoo fouled out. Florida State advanced to the final, 79-75.

In the UCLA-Louisville game, teacher gave student another lesson: You may know the tricks, but you also have to have the talent. Although Price played great for Coach Crum, Walton was the difference in this contest, scoring 33 points and getting 21 rebounds. The Bruins moved on to their sixth straight championship game, 96-77.

Florida State coach Hugh Durham knew his chances of beating UCLA were slim. He also realized that he would have no chance if he let the Bruins dictate the style of play. So right after the opening tip, the Seminoles ignited a run-and-gun offense that caught the Bruins by surprise. Each time Florida State got the ball, the players raced upcourt and took the first decent-looking shot they saw. In no time, they were ahead 21-14. The UCLA defense put a stop to this nonsense, and the Bruins quickly tied the score. By halftime, they were on top 50-39.

Wilkes, Bibby, and Walton provided most of the offense in the second half, as UCLA continued to add to its lead. Florida State's last chance came when Walton picked up his fourth foul and took a seat with 6 minutes left. The Seminoles cut the lead by more than half but ran out of time. Undefeated UCLA had won the NCAA championship again, this time by a score of 81-76.

Champion: UCLA
Winning Coach: John Wooden
Number of Schools in Tournament: 25
Best Player: Bill Walton, UCLA

Tiny Otto Petty elevates past UNC's George Karl, Dennis Wuycik, and Bob McAdoo in the national semifinal. Petty could not repeat his stellar performance against UCLA in the title game.

1973
Indiana Hoosiers
Memphis State Tigers
Providence Friars
UCLA Bruins

What can you possibly do to improve on a perfect season? All you can do is be perfect again. This was the goal for John Wooden and the UCLA Bruins as they headed into the 1972–1973 campaign. Bill Walton was back for his junior year, along with Keith Wilkes. Greg Lee, a junior, stepped into Henry Bibby's role as floor leader. Also on the squad were Larry Farmer, Larry Hollyfield, and a trio of backups—Dave Meyers, Swen Nater, and Tommy Curtis—who would have been stars for any other school. As far as Wooden was concerned, this was his best team ever—and they proved it by going through another season without a loss.

This was bad news for the other Final Four teams, each of which had excellent players. The Hoosiers, under fiery second-year coach Bobby Knight, had three excellent players in Steve Downing, Steve Green, and Quinn Buckner. Providence, coached by Dave Gavitt, drove opponents mad with guards Ernie DiGregorio and Kevin Stacom and center Marvin Barnes. Gene Bartow's Memphis State squad had the lethal trio of Larry Kenon, Larry Finch, and Ronnie Robinson.

For an impatient man, Coach Knight had a very patient team. He told his players to take their time and to work the ball around until a good scoring opportunity emerged—after all, even UCLA gave up easy shots from time to time. In the semifinal, the Hoosiers and Bruins traded baskets for a few minutes, and Indiana took a 20-17 lead. Knight was looking like a genius. Then the roof caved in. UCLA went on an 18-0 tear, with Walton snatching loose balls and rebounds and firing long outlet passes to start the fast break. The score at halftime was 40-22, Bruins. In the second half, Wooden decided to rest his key players. Curtis came off the bench to score 22 points, proving again how deep the UCLA squad was. Despite a late run by Indiana, the Bruins won 70-59.

Providence, playing without Barnes (who had not recovered from a knee injury suffered in the previous game), gave Memphis State all it could handle in the other semifinal. The Friars raced to a 49-40 halftime lead on the shoulders of the pesky DiGregorio, who scored 36 points. Without Barnes, however, Providence could not stop Robinson and Kenon. The Tigers battled back in the second half and won 98-85.

From the outset of the championship game, there was something a little different about Walton. He appeared more intense, more focused. He demanded the ball on offense, and Lee was all too happy to oblige. Fighting off double- and triple-teams, "Big Red" seemed to hit every shot he took. Memphis State was playing well, too. Although Walton contained Robinson, Kenon and Finch were able to get to the hoop, and the Tigers' zone was effective against the other UCLA shooters. At halftime, the score was tied 37-37.

The first 9 minutes of the second half decided the game. Walton scored 14 points during the span to give UCLA a big lead. He continued his spectacular performance until, with 3 minutes left, he was forced to leave the game with a leg injury. As Walton limped to the bench, Finch congratulated

Bill Walton slides into position against Indiana during the 1973 semifinals. UCLA won the game handily.

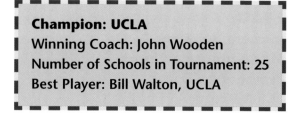

Champion: UCLA
Winning Coach: John Wooden
Number of Schools in Tournament: 25
Best Player: Bill Walton, UCLA

1974

Kansas Jayhawks
Marquette Warriors
North Carolina State Wolfpack
UCLA Bruins

There was not much to say about UCLA's seven consecutive NCAA titles—unless you lived in Raleigh, North Carolina. Fans and students of North Carolina State University believed that their Wolfpack had been the best team in basketball during the 1972–73 season. Despite a 27-0 record, they had not been allowed to participate in the NCAA Tournament because of recruiting violations. The two teams met early in the 1973–74 season, and UCLA won. After that meeting, however, the Bruins lost to Notre Dame (ending a record 88-game winning streak) and then lost twice more in the same weekend to Pac 10 rivals Oregon and Oregon State. When the Bruins and the Wolfpack made it to the Final Four, the college basketball world braced for a war.

The Bruins had another excellent team. Dave Meyers and Tommy Curtis joined the starting lineup, along with Bill Walton, Keith Wilkes, and Greg Lee. On the bench were talented Andre McCarter and Marques Johnson. NC State had the game's most dynamic player, David Thompson. A 6-foot-4 guard with a 4-foot vertical leap, he could pick a quarter off the top of a backboard and touch the rim with his head. He also happened to be a great shooter and ball handler,

him, and both players got a huge ovation. The game ended 87-66, Bruins. Walton had hit an amazing 21 of 22 shots and finished with 44 points—the most ever in an NCAA championship game.

as well as a first-rate defender. Thompson's supporting cast featured 7-foot-4 Tom Burleson, 5-foot-6 Monte Towe, and power forward Tim Stoddard, who later gained fame as a pitcher for the Baltimore Orioles. Almost forgotten were the other two Final Four participants—one of whom would advance to the championship game. Kansas relied on the leadership of point guard Tom Kivisto, while Marquette boasted the trio of Maurice Lucas, Marcus Washington, and Maurice Ellis.

The first semifinal was played in an atmosphere that was more like a heavyweight boxing championship than a basketball game. UCLA and NC State slugged it out in the first half and went into the locker room even on points, 35-35. The first big blow of the match was landed early in the second half, by Walton. He had been battering the stick-thin Burleson all game long, and now it was beginning to show. Walton led a scoring spurt that resulted in a seemingly insurmountable 11-point lead. Thompson brought the Wolfpack back, however, and they tied the score again, 65-65. As time ran out, Stoddard had an open jumper to win, but it clanked off the rim and the game went into overtime.

Both squads slowed things down in the extra period, and this resulted in a grand total of one basket each. In the second overtime, Walton and Wilkes appeared to blow the game open with seven straight points. Then, incredibly, NC State responded with 11 unanswered points of its own. The key to the comeback was the scrambling, desperate Wolfpack defense. For the first time in a decade, Wooden watched as his Bruins lost their composure and completely fell apart. UCLA was finally beaten, 80-77.

The right to face Thompson in the final belonged to Marquette, which had defeated Kansas 76-64 on a strong effort from Lucas. The Warriors held their own against the Wolfpack in the championship game, and even led late in the first half. Then coach Al McGuire was ejected for arguing with the referees, and his team lost its heart. NC State built a double-digit lead that it never

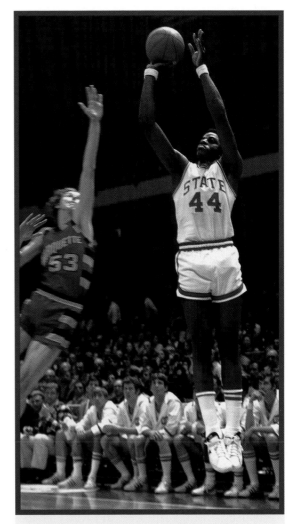

David Thompson squeezes off a jumper against Marquette. Thompson led all tournament scorers with 97 points.

relinquished. Thompson scored 21 points and Burleson blocked seven shots in a 76-64 win.

> **Champion: North Carolina State**
> **Winning Coach: Norm Sloan**
> **Number of Schools in Tournament: 25**
> **Best Player: David Thompson,**
> **North Carolina State**

1975
Louisville Cardinals
Kentucky Wildcats
Syracuse Orangemen
UCLA Bruins

Those who assumed that UCLA was dead found there was plenty of life and plenty of fight left in the Bruins. Coaching his final season, John Wooden led his team to a 23-3 record despite losing Bill Walton, who was the first choice in the 1974 NBA Draft. The 1974–75 squad was reminiscent of the teams sandwiched between Walton and Lew Alcindor—solid but hardly spectacular. Dave Meyers, Richard Washington, and Pete Trgovich turned in steady, workman-like performances night in and night out, while sophomore Marques Johnson provided some pizzazz off the bench.

The other schools at the Big Dance seemed every bit as good as UCLA. Sharp-shooting Louisville, with Junior Bridgeman and Allen Murphy, had lost only twice. Syracuse, starring Jim Lee and Rudy Hackett, had advanced with impressive victories over Rutgers, Cincinnati, and Maryland. Kentucky returned to the Final Four for the first time since its 1966 loss to Texas Western.

Wooden and Denny Crum faced off in a big game for the second time in four seasons, but this time Crum felt he had the more talented team. The athletic Cardinals ran UCLA ragged in the first half, and Murphy scored at will in the low post. The Bruins clawed their way back into the game, however, and finished the first half trailing only, 37-33. The game stayed close throughout the second half, with Washington stepping up and scoring clutch baskets for UCLA. He sank a pair of free throws with a minute left to cut Louisville's lead to two, and then Johnson swooped in and stole the inbound pass. The future superstar calmly scored the tying basket, and the game went into overtime. Louisville went up 74-73 with 50 seconds remaining, and Crum called a time-out. He instructed his players to run out the clock with a four-corner stall and inserted an extra ball handler, Terry Howard, into the game.

Wooden told the Bruins to foul Howard. The UCLA coach knew Howard was an excellent free-throw shooter but gambled that he might be tight coming off the bench. Wooden's eyes grew wide as Howard missed and Washington came down with the rebound. The Bruins rushed up the court, and the ball went back to Washington on the baseline. From 12 feet away, he sank the game-winning jumper. It was as close a call as Wooden had ever experienced as a coach.

In the other semifinal, Kentucky's "Clydesdales" trampled Syracuse 95-79. The Wildcats got their nickname because they were big and powerful, and they could run. Center Rick Robey and guard Kevin Grevey were the team's go-to guys, but in this game it was forward Goose Givens who led both teams with 24 points.

John Wooden, rolled-up program in hand, signals to his players during his final game as a coach.

1976
Indiana Hoosiers
Michigan Wolverines
Rutgers Scarlet Knights
UCLA Bruins

There was no lack of young coaches to replace John Wooden as "best in the business" after he left UCLA. Chief among them was Bobby Knight of Indiana. A member of the great Ohio State teams of the early 1960s, he took a coaching job at the U.S. Military Academy at West Point and whipped the Cadets into consistent winners. Knight was hired by the Hoosiers for the 1971–72 season and lost only 20 games in his first four seasons. In 1975–76, he assembled one of the great teams in history. Quinn Buckner and Bobby Wilkerson made up the back-court, Kent Benson was the center, and Tom Abernathy and Scott May—the team's best player—were the forwards. Knight preached unquestioning discipline and dedication. He demanded teamwork on offense and relentless hard work on defense. The Hoosiers could beat you in a dozen different ways, and in this great year they beat everyone.

The other Final Four participants in 1976 were wary of the Hoosiers but not scared. Each had plenty of talent. UCLA, with Gene Bartow calling the shots, had Marques Johnson, Richard Washington, and Andre McCarter back, along with newcomers Ray Townsend and David Greenwood. Rutgers featured Phil Sellers, Eddie Jordan,

With his players determined to send him out a winner, Coach Wooden knew he had the emotional edge in the final. The Bruins came out flying. They hit shots from everywhere. The Wildcats bent a bit but did not break. They kept pace with UCLA, trailing by only three points at the half. The first break in the game came when Robey had to leave with foul problems. With more room to operate inside, the Bruins extended their lead to seven. Kentucky never made up the difference, and UCLA won a most unexpected and gratifying championship, 92-85.

Bobby Knight plans strategy during a time-out. His Hoosiers won the NCAA title and finished the year a perfect 32-0.

the court confident that they would defend their championship. Once this game started, however, it was clear that the outcome would be far different. Abernathy completely outplayed Washington, while Wilkerson dished out 7 assists and crashed the boards for a remarkable 19 rebounds. Wherever UCLA turned, an Indiana player was already there. The Hoosiers prevailed, 65-51.

Michigan coach Johnny Orr was well aware of how dangerous Indiana was. His Wolverines had already lost to the Hoosiers twice that year. Orr needed a break in this game, and it appeared he got one early in the first half. Wilkerson, the senior playmaker, collided with another player and was knocked unconscious. While Knight and the Hoosiers came to grips with their predicament, Michigan rolled to a 35-29 halftime lead.

In the locker room, the Indiana players braced for one of Coach Knight's legendary tirades. Instead, he spoke calmly and clearly. There were 20 minutes left to play, he said. They had that much time to show their true colors.

Knight's talk worked wonders. May and Benson kept Michigan off the boards, and Buckner hounded the Wolverines' guards to the brink of exhaustion. Jim Wisman and Jim Crews, filling in for Wilkerson, combined for 10 assists. Indiana outscored Michigan by 24 points in the second half, and won the game 86-68 to finish the year at a perfect 32-0.

and Mike Dabney. And Michigan was powered by Ricky Green, Phil Hubbard, and Steve Grote.

Rutgers, undefeated going into its semifinal confrontation with Michigan, looked to Sellers whenever it needed a big bucket. In this game, however, the shifty 6-foot-5 senior was ice-cold. Dabney and Jordan were not much better, and Coach Tom Young watched in frustration as the Wolverines buried the Scarlet Knights, 86-70.

The Hoosiers, meanwhile, had to get past UCLA. After cruising through their first three tournament games, the Bruins hit

Champion: Indiana
Winning Coach: Bobby Knight
Number of Schools in Tournament: 32
Best Player: Kent Benson, Indiana

1977

Marquette Warriors
North Carolina Tar Heels
North Carolina-Charlotte 49ers
Nevada-Las Vegas Runnin' Rebels

One of the fun things about the Final Four is the history behind the matchups. How teams have done against one another in the past adds to the excitement and anticipation. In 1977, there was absolutely no history to the Final Four. None of the teams had ever faced the others, so it was anyone's guess who would win the NCAA championship. UNLV, under Coach Jerry Tarkanian, had a wide-open attack that featured six players capable of scoring 20 or more a game. Reggie Theus and Glen "Gonzo" Gondrezick were the two best, but Eddie Owens, Robert Smith, Sam Smith, and Larry Moffett were dangerous, too. NC-Charlotte had Cedric Maxwell, a power forward whose hands were like magnets when it came to rebounds and loose balls. Dean Smith's Tar Heels had a dynamite trio of open-court players in Phil Ford, Mike O'Koren, and Walter Davis. And Marquette had great balance with Butch Lee at guard, Bo Ellis at forward, and Jerome Whitehead at center. Their coach, Al McGuire, had announced that he would retire at season's end. Initially, this news threw the Warriors into a tailspin. By the time they reached the tournament, however, it served as a common bond. They wanted to send "Irish Al" out a winner, as the UCLA Bruins had done for John Wooden two seasons before.

With no clue as to how these teams would fare against one another, fans were pleasantly surprised when the two semifinals were decided by a total of three points.

In the opening game, Theus and Tony Smith gave UNLV a 49-43 halftime advantage. In the second half, O'Koren and Davis led a Carolina comeback, and the Tar Heels regained the lead with 16 minutes to play. Coach Smith then ordered his players to go into his famous four-corners stall. The

Butch Lee backs his way toward the hoop against NC-Charlotte in the 1977 semifinal. He was named the tournament's Most Outstanding Player.

impatient Rebels tried to force the action, but this resulted in several easy "backdoor" layups for UNC. UNLV got close but never caught the Tar Heels, who won 84-83.

In the other semifinal, the 49ers gave the Warriors all they could handle. Marquette took an early lead on the inside scoring of Whitehead, but Lee and Ellis could not find the basket. This enabled NC-Charlotte to creep back to within three points at the intermission. Maxwell demolished the Warriors in the second half, hitting short jumpers and scoring on offensive rebounds. With 5 seconds left and the game tied, McGuire called for time and sketched out a play—a long pass to Ellis. The ball came inbounds but was tipped in the air by one of the 49ers. With time running out, Whitehead grabbed the loose ball and drove to the basket for the winning score for Marquette in a 51-49 heartstopper.

Knowing that the Tar Heels would try to control the tempo if they got a lead, the Warriors came out strong in the first half of the final. Ellis and Whitehead swept up all the rebounds; guard Jim Boylan shadowed Ford wherever he went; and Marquette scored often enough to hold the lead. The second half saw O'Koren break out, and within 7 minutes Carolina had regained the lead. Smith signaled for the four corners, but the Warriors were ready. They sagged back and lured the Tar Heels into taking a poor shot. After grabbing the rebound, Marquette got the ball to Lee, who sunk the go-ahead basket. When Carolina could not catch up, they had to start fouling. The Warriors made their shots and pulled away for a 67-59 victory. On the Marquette bench, McGuire bowed his head and wept for joy.

> **Champion: Marquette**
> **Winning Coach: Al McGuire**
> **Number of Schools in Tournament: 32**
> **Best Player: Butch Lee, Marquette**

1978
Arkansas Razorbacks
Duke Blue Devils
Kentucky Wildcats
Notre Dame Fighting Irish

The ghost of Adolph Rupp, who passed away in 1977, both inspired and haunted the Kentucky Wildcats during the 1977–1978 season. The team seemed determined to bring a championship banner to Rupp Arena, and as they neared the end of the season, the players began to feel that anything less than an NCAA title would be a monumental failure. Under coach Joe B. Hall, the Wildcats had grown up and improved since their loss to UCLA two years earlier. Rick Robey and Goose Givens were the senior leaders; Kyle Macy, the floor general; and James Lee and Mike Phillips, the team's top defenders.

To win it all, the Wildcats would have to contend with three big-time basketball programs. Duke had a young, smart team starring Mike Gminski, Gene Banks, and Jim Spanarkel. Notre Dame, coached by Digger Phelps, featured Kelly Tripucka, Rich Branning, Duck Williams, and Bill Laimbeer. Eddie Sutton's Arkansas Razorbacks starred ball-hawk Sidney Moncrief, Ron Brewer, and Marvin Delph.

Moncrief and company challenged the Wildcats in the first semifinal with a tight man-to-man defense, but when the team got into foul trouble, Coach Sutton had to switch to a zone. Givens found a seam in the zone and started drilling short jumpers. The halftime score was only 32-30, Kentucky, but the Wildcats now had the momentum. Kentucky raced to a 9-point lead in the second half, which forced Sutton to unleash Moncrief, Brewer, and Delph in an all-out defensive attack. The strategy worked, as Arkansas pulled within one basket with a couple of minutes left. The Razorbacks needed one more big defensive play to take control of the game, but Givens slithered through their full-court press for an uncontested layup. Kentucky went on to win 64-59.

In the other semifinal, Bill Foster's Duke team bombed the Fighting Irish in the first half, with Banks and Gminski hitting shots from all over the court. The Blue Devils maintained a double-digit lead until the final minutes of the game, when Notre Dame launched an incredible comeback. They pulled within 2 but could get no closer, and lost 90-86.

According to the experts, the championship game would boil down to a battle under the backboards: Robey and Phillips versus Gminski and Kenny Dennard. To stop Kentucky, Coach Foster set up a special zone that kept three Blue Devils near the basket at all times. This opened up a spot on the floor near the foul line that could not be defended. Once again, it was Givens who found this seam and began hitting short jumpers. He scored the last 16 points of the first half for Kentucky, which took a 45-38 lead into the locker room. When the teams returned to the court, Duke stuck to its zone. Givens kept shooting, and the ball kept going in. The senior finished the game with 41 points, and Kentucky won 94-88.

Champion: Kentucky
Winning Coach: Joe Hall
Number of Schools in Tournament: 32
Best Player: Goose Givens, Kentucky

Kentucky's James Lee puts the final nail in Duke's coffin with a slam dunk in the championship game.

THE MIRACLE WORKERS

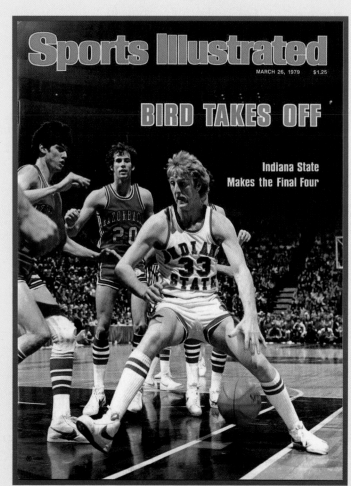

Larry Bird and Magic Johnson were college basketball's two most intense competitors in the late 1970s—they even competed for magazine covers! Bird was the game's greatest one-man show.

Basketball was in trouble in the spring of 1979. In the NBA, empty arenas and widespread drug use threatened to destroy the sport. The league's three "anchor" franchises—the New York Knicks, the Los Angeles Lakers, and the Boston Celtics—were playing poorly. Television executives were actually wondering whether it was even worth airing the NBA Finals live.

College ball was not doing much better. Because UCLA had won the NCAA championship so many times in the past, a generation of fans grew up thinking there was no drama in the college game. Also, due to a wave of recruiting violations, too many schools had been put on probation. Every week, it seemed, another big-time program was embroiled in a scandal.

Enter Magic Johnson and Larry Bird, a couple of squeaky-clean superstars who embodied everything that was great about basketball. Johnson, a sophomore, was the 6-foot-9 point guard for the Michigan State Spartans. He towered over defenders and flicked perfect passes all over the court—all the while flashing his million-dollar smile. A media-savvy kid from the industrial town of Lansing, Michigan, Johnson represented the promise of the future. Bird, a senior forward for Indiana State, was a throwback to the old days, when a single star could dominate a game, often through his own sheer will. He described himself as the "Hick from French Lick"—French Lick, Indiana, was his hometown.

At first glance, these young men could not have been more different. Yet as they closed in on a championship confrontation, fans realized that in two ways they were exactly the same. Johnson and Bird loved basketball, and they loved winning even more.

The Michigan State-Indiana State final recaptured college basketball's lost audience and then some. Because the championship game was being held on a Monday night instead of a Sunday afternoon, millions of people went to school and work that day and started choosing sides in the Magic-Bird rivalry. By game time, a record number of viewers had settled in front of their TVs.

As this *Sports Illustrated* shows, Magic Johnson brought skills to the point guard position that made him impossible to handle. He could pass, shoot, dribble, and finish fast breaks with thunderous dunks.

A few weeks later, Johnson and Bird moved to the NBA. Bird had actually been selected the year before in a controversial move by the Celtics. Johnson was taken by the Lakers, who had traded for the first pick in the 1979 draft. As if scripted by a Hollywood writer, Bird won the Rookie of the Year award, while Johnson led Los Angeles to the NBA championship. Their rivalry reenergized professional basketball and turned the world back on to the unique thrills of college hoops.

1979

DePaul Blue Demons
Indiana State Sycamores
Michigan State Spartans
Pennsylvania Quakers

One of the toughest trivia questions in college basketball is "Who were the 'other' teams in the 1979 Final Four besides Michigan State and Indiana State?" The answer is Penn and DePaul. With the Magic Johnson–led Spartans on a collision course with the Larry Bird–led Sycamores, almost no attention was paid to the Quakers and the Blue Demons. Penn reached the semifinals on the strength of its disciplined defense and the leadership of Tony Price and Tim Smith. DePaul, coached by the legendary Ray Meyer, had a dangerous team featuring the sensational Mark Aguirre, Gary Garland, and Curtis Watkins.

Unbeaten Indiana State was reminiscent of teams from the 1940s and 1950s, with one unstoppable superstar surrounded by solid role players. Michigan State was a team that relied on the momentum created by Johnson. His running mate, Greg Kelser, specialized in rim-rattling alley-oop dunks.

Penn's defense had worked wonders against its fellow Ivy League schools. It had also served the Quakers well in tournament upsets over North Carolina, Syracuse, and St. John's. Against the fast break of Jud Heathcote's Spartans, however, it was useless. When Magic and company were not slicing through the Quakers, they were jumping over them. The game's halftime score of 50-17 represented the biggest lead any team had ever taken into intermission in Final Four play. Johnson recorded a "triple-double," with 29 points, 10 rebounds, and 10 assists, in Michigan State's 101-67 victory.

The other semifinal was much closer. The last time DePaul had advanced this far in the NCAA Tournament was during World War II, and Coach Meyer (who was coaching the team back then!) had every confidence his team could handle Bird. After the All-American gave Indiana State an 11-point lead in the second half, the Blue Demons put on the defensive pressure and got back in the game. In the final minutes, the lead seesawed back and forth. The contest turned when Bird grabbed a rebound and fired an outlet pass to guard Carl Nicks, who rifled the ball to a wide-open Bob Heaton for an easy layup. DePaul blew its chance to tie the game when Garland passed up an easy jumper and passed the ball to Aguirre, who missed a 20-footer. The Sycamores held on for a 76-74 victory.

The hype surrounding the final—which for the first time was held on a Monday evening—was incredible. For several days, features on Bird and Johnson had been running on television and in the newspapers. By game time, millions of people who had never watched a minute of college basketball in their lives were tuned in to see which superstar would prevail. A slight edge was given to Michigan State, mainly because Bird was nursing a sore thumb. His shooting, passing, and ballhandling were crucial to the Sycamores' success—and the injury was hurting far more than he cared to admit.

This became obvious in the early stages of the game, when Bird missed several shots that he normally made. Meanwhile, the Spartans were getting open shots and hitting them. Johnson was drawing two defenders almost every time down the court, and he had no trouble finding unguarded teammates with pinpoint passes. The Spartans led by 9 at intermission, and they

Larry Bird tries to "thread the needle" between Michigan State defenders Magic Johnson and Jay Vincent during the 1979 NCAA championship game.

increased that lead as Bird continued to struggle with his shooting in the second half. Nicks picked up some of the slack, but every time Indiana State seemed ready to put together a run, Michigan State made a basket to halt the comeback. The final score, 75-64, makes the game look closer than it was; the Spartans were in command for the full 40 minutes.

Champion: Michigan State
Winning Coach: Jud Heathcote
Number of Schools in Tournament: 40
Best Player: Magic Johnson,
Michigan State

THE 1980s

1980

Iowa Hawkeyes
Louisville Cardinals
Purdue Boilermakers
UCLA Bruins

The NCAA Tournament had a different look in 1980 thanks to a couple of important changes. First, schools were made to cut back on the number of basketball scholarships they could offer. Second, the tournament field was expanded from 40 to 48 teams. The combined effect of these new rules was that smaller schools could better compete with the big programs for the nation's top talent—and could compete in the tournament itself. Also, good teams that had been squeezed out of the draw in the past were now invited to fill the extra spots. Of the Final Four participants, only one, Louisville, would have even qualified the year before!

The Cardinals, still coached by Denny Crum, had raised the slam dunk to an art form. Darrell Griffith, nicknamed "Dr. Dunkenstein," led a high-flying crew that also featured hardworking support players like guard Jerry Eaves and freshman forward Rodney McCray. UCLA was back in the Final Four thanks to first-year coach

Larry Brown. An All-Star player and title-winning coach in the ABA, Brown knew better than most what it took to be a champion. His team featured high-scoring Kiki Vandeweghe, swingman Mike Sanders, and Rocket Rod Foster, a mercurial freshman point guard. Iowa boasted the solid trio of Ronnie Lester, Kenny Arnold, and Vince Brookins, while Purdue was led by center Joe Barry Carroll.

The spotlight was on Griffith and Lester in the first semifinal. The Hawkeyes, fearful of Griffith's driving ability, sagged back and gave him the outside shot. To their dismay, he hit one long bomb after another. Things went from bad to worse when Lester, who had been perfect from the field, went down with a knee injury and did not return. Arnold shouldered the scoring load for Iowa in the second half, but it was not enough to overcome Griffith's great shooting and the grunt work of McCray. The Cardinals prevailed, 80-72.

In its game against Purdue, UCLA decided that the best way to control Carroll was to smother him in defenders. The frustrated big man was limited to just 14 shots. Meanwhile, Purdue's trapping defense was ineffective against the Bruins. Although overmatched in terms of size, Brown's troops were quicker than their opponents. UCLA nursed a small lead throughout the game, and then made their free throws when the Boilermakers were forced to start fouling in the final minutes. The final score was 67-62.

The championship game was a matchup of two young, enthusiastic teams and two protégés of famous coaches. Crum, an assistant for John Wooden, was looking for an NCAA title in his third Final Four. Brown, who played for Dean Smith in North Carolina, was within one victory of the summit in his very first year as a college coach. At midseason, Brown had promoted guards Foster and Michael Holton—both freshmen—into the starting lineup. This controversial move had worked, but no one knew how they would respond to guarding Louisville's Griffith and Eaves. Everyone seemed edgy in the early going—everyone, that is, except Griffith. A monstrous jam and a few swishes from outside got him warmed up, and he gave the Bruins all they could handle in the first half. The rest of the Cardinals were of little help. UCLA managed to hit a few shots, and at halftime the Bruins were actually ahead 28-26. In the locker room, Crum ripped into his players. Then he felt bad and apologized; the coach realized they knew how bad they had been—and how good they could be.

The Cardinals' play improved in the second half, but UCLA still held a 4-point lead with just 4 minutes to play. When Vandeweghe stole a pass and glided toward the basket, it looked as if the Bruins would break the game open. Then, out of nowhere, came Eaves to obstruct the shot, and teammate Willie Brown swooped in for the rebound. On each of Louisville's next two possessions, Griffith made pretty passes to

Poncho Wright (left) congratulates teammate Darrell Griffith after the 1980 title game. His jumper with minutes to play gave Louisville a lead it never relinquished.

Eaves, who hit his shots to knot the score at 54-54. Griffith then gave the Cardinals the lead with a jump shot. Louisville scored the game's last 11 points to turn a 54-48 deficit into an incredible 59-54 win.

Champion: Louisville
Winning Coach: Denny Crum
Number of Schools in Tournament: 48
Best Player: Darrell Griffith, Louisville

1981
Indiana Hoosiers
LSU Tigers
North Carolina Tar Heels
Virginia Cavaliers

In the spring of 1979, Chicago high-school star Isiah Thomas announced he would attend Indiana University. This raised plenty of eyebrows in the college basketball world. Thomas was a player who liked to "go with the flow" and experiment during games. Bobby Knight, who coached the Hoosiers, was a disciplinarian who would not tolerate this kind of precociousness. This "Odd Couple," as they were often called, found they had one important thing in common: They loved to win. By Thomas's sophomore year, he had gotten used to Knight's tirades, and the coach had grown accustomed to his point guard's creativity on the court. With a supporting cast that included Landon Turner, Ray Tolbert, and Randy Wittman, the Hoosiers were the team to beat for the 1981 championship.

Standing in their path were Dale Brown's Tigers, Dean Smith's Tar Heels, and Terry Holland's Cavaliers. Carolina and Virginia would be the biggest challenges for the Hoosiers, but luckily for Indiana they played each other in the semifinals. Virginia had 7-foot-4 center Ralph Sampson, "the best big man since Bill Walton," and clutch-shooting Jeff Lamp; UNC had a trio of stars in James Worthy, Sam Perkins, and Al Wood.

In the first Final Four contest, LSU played surprisingly well against Indiana's front line and actually led at the half, 30-27. Were it not for Thomas's superb play, the situation would have been far worse. Thomas got into foul trouble in the second half, but Turner picked up the slack with

several clutch shots. Jim Thomas, Isiah's replacement, played beautifully in his place, and Indiana won 67-49.

In the other game, the Tar Heels neutralized Sampson by placing Worthy in front of him and Perkins behind him. On offense, Wood hit 14 of 19 shots and 11 of 13 free throws for 39 points, and also hauled down 10 rebounds. The teams were tied 27-27 at

Bobby Knight confers with Isiah Thomas. Though stormy at times, their relationship delivered an NCAA crown to Indiana in 1981.

halftime, but when Lamp cooled off in the second half, Carolina pulled away for a 78-65 win.

The championship game hinged on Indiana's ability to control Worthy, Perkins, and Wood. In the opening minutes, it looked like the Hoosiers were in trouble. Each seemed at the top of his game. To make matters worse, Isiah Thomas was ice-cold. Knight reshuffled his deck and brought in Jim Thomas to shadow Wood. This move not only worked, but also created a matchup problem for the Tar Heels. One of their forwards now had to guard Wittman, a lethal outside shooter. By halftime, Indiana had caught up and was ahead by one point. In the second half, Turner and Tolbert clamped down on Perkins and Worthy, and Isiah rediscovered his shooting touch. Indiana won, 63-50, to give Coach Knight his second championship.

> **Champion: Indiana**
> **Winning Coach: Bobby Knight**
> **Number of Schools in Tournament: 48**
> **Best Player: Isiah Thomas, Indiana**

1982
Georgetown Hoyas
Houston Cougars
Louisville Cardinals
North Carolina Tar Heels

Sometimes it takes a few years for fans to appreciate a great Final Four. Once in a while, they realize how good it is from the moment it starts. In 1982, four dynamic teams competed for the college crown. The Houston Cougars were led by Clyde Drexler, Larry Micheaux, and an unknown freshman center from Nigeria named Hakeem Olajuwon.

Louisville, with Derek Smith, Lancaster Gordon, and Charles Jones joining 1980 holdovers Rodney McCray and Jerry Eaves, had a superb starting five. Georgetown, a monstrous defensive team coached by former Celtic John Thompson, combined the smoothness of guard "Sleepy" Floyd and the raw power of another foreign-born freshman center, Patrick Ewing, who had emigrated from Jamaica in the 1970s. Dean Smith's Tar Heels had James Worthy and Sam Perkins back, along with a cool and clever freshman guard named Michael Jordan.

In a memorable contest, North Carolina faced Houston for the right to advance to the championship game. Although the Tar Heels were athletic enough to run with the fast-breaking Cougars, Coach Smith preferred to slow the game down and work for good scoring chances. He was pleased when Worthy, Perkins, and Jordan shot extremely well. Meanwhile, Micheaux and Larry Rose were hot for Houston. The Cougars went into the locker room with a 31-29 halftime lead. The chess match continued in the second half, as Carolina hit clutch shots but Houston did not. The lead swung to the Tar Heels, and they held on for a masterful 68-63 victory.

Coach Thompson borrowed a page from Dean Smith's book by slowing the game down in his meeting with Denny Crum and Louisville. Floyd and fellow guard Fred Brown walked the ball up the court on offense and challenged the Cardinals' guards from the baseline to mid-court. Neither team shot very well in the first half, which ended with the Hoyas ahead 24-22. This was Georgetown's kind of game. In the second half, they tightened the noose and outscored Louisville by 2 points again. The Cardinals' fast break never got off the ground, and they lost 50-46.

James Worthy contests a shot by Patrick Ewing. Both players shot exceptionally well in a tight defensive battle.

Sportswriters had plenty to write about before the final. Coaches Smith and Thompson were longtime friends. Worthy and Floyd had played ball together when they were kids growing up in rural North Carolina. And then there were the two quiet freshmen, Jordan and Ewing. They oozed with the kind of talent that could blow a game wide open. Georgetown began the contest with a tight zone that funneled the ball toward Ewing, who swatted away anything the Tar Heels put up. Carolina adjusted and came back to tie the score at 18-18. From that point on, neither team opened up much of a lead. Midway through the second half, the Tar Heels seemed to grab the momentum when Floyd blew an open layup and Worthy followed with a thunderous dunk at the other end. With less than a minute left, however, Floyd gave Georgetown a 62-61 lead with a spectacular off-balance jumper.

Coach Smith called time-out and designed a play. He knew the Hoyas would expect the ball to go inside to Worthy, so he called Jordan's number 23 instead. The freshman took the ball to the left wing and calmly swished a 16-footer. With time ticking away, Thompson motioned his players to attack Carolina's defense before the Tar Heels could get set. Brown dribbled quickly across midcourt, then heard Eric Smith call for the ball. Smith made a great cut to the basket, leaving Worthy all by himself in the middle of the court. Brown, obviously nervous, mistook Worthy for his teammate and flipped him the ball. The game ended moments later, 63-62. After 20 unsuccessful tries—including six Final Four appearances—Dean Smith finally had his first national championship.

> **Champion: North Carolina**
> **Winning Coach: Dean Smith**
> **Number of Schools in Tournament: 48**
> **Best Player: James Worthy,**
> **North Carolina**

1983
Georgia Bulldogs
Houston Cougars
Louisville Cardinals
North Carolina State Wolfpack

Although it is extremely rare for a low seed to reach the Final Four, it happens often enough that no team can ever be counted out. North Carolina State is perhaps the best example of this. Coached by emotional Jim Valvano, the Wolfpack lost 10 games in 1982–83 and was not being considered for a tournament bid. They got into the draw only after upsetting several teams to win the Atlantic Coast Conference tournament. Then they managed to reach the Final Four with heart-stopping wins over Pepperdine, UNLV, and Virginia. Valvano's team was a collection of no-names, including Sidney Lowe, Thurl Bailey, Dereck Whittenburg, Lorenzo Charles, and Cozell McQueen.

By comparison, the other Final Four teams were loaded with talent. Georgia had Vern Fleming, James Banks, and Terry Fair; Louisville had the McCray brothers, Rodney and Scooter, along with Milt Wagner and Lancaster Gordon; and Houston—the tournament favorite—had Clyde Drexler, Hakeem Olajuwon, Larry Micheaux, Alvin Franklin, and Michael Young. The Cougars dunked so often that they began calling themselves the "Phi Slamma Jamma" fraternity.

The Cardinals figured they could keep up with Houston's high-wire act—and for most of the game, they were right. The fans were treated to an explosive exhibition of above-the-rim basketball, as Louisville took a 5-point lead into the locker room after 20 minutes. In the second half, the Cardinals shifted into a lower gear while the Cougars went into overdrive. In an unbelievable dunk fest, they outscored Louisville 20-0 and held on to win 94-81. In the second semifinal, Georgia tried to run on plodding NC State. Only Fleming seemed to be in sync, however, and the Wolfpack hung tough. Whittenburg, Lowe, and Bailey hit their shots, and Valvano watched as his troops produced a grinding 67-60 win.

Cozell McQueen is on top of the world after NC State's buzzer-beating upset of Houston. The 1983 NCAA Final still stands as the most heart-stopping conclusion in tournament history.

Prior to the final, Valvano and his players discussed their chances. They agreed that the only way to win was to keep the score low. And the way you did that against the Cougars was to keep them "grounded." That meant fighting for position, getting in their way, and preventing the outlet passes that ignited their fast break. When asked what he thought the key to victory would be, overconfident Houston coach Guy Lewis predicted the team "with the most dunks" would win. The Wolfpack executed Valvano's game plan to perfection in the first half and built an 8-point lead by intermission. Only Olajuwon was scoring in Houston's half-court offense, and the Cougars went the full 20 minutes without a single dunk. In the locker room, Coach Lewis made his players realize that NC State was simply not going to let them run. It was time, he said, to concentrate on winning the old-fashioned way. And concentrate they did—Houston opened the half with a 17-2 run and took a 7-point lead.

Hoping to rest his skinny center for a few minutes, Lewis benched Olajuwon. This move backfired, as the Houston offense went cold. At the same time, Whittenburg, Lowe, and reserve Terry Gannon began swishing long jumpers. By the time Olajuwon was hustled back into the game, the Cougars had been sapped of their confidence. Valvano instructed his players to start fouling, and Houston, a terrible free-throw-shooting team, began throwing up bricks. The Wolfpack tied the score at 52-52 on a 24-footer by Whittenburg, then purposely fouled Franklin. He missed his free throw; NC State got the rebound and began setting up for the game's final shot. Houston played tight defense and kept the Wolfpack out at the perimeter. Whittenburg had the

ball on the left wing, then lost the handle. He scampered after the ball and, realizing he only had a few seconds, threw a prayer up from 30 feet. All 10 players watched the ball arc toward the basket, but only one had a plan. Lorenzo Charles, who had slipped behind Olajuwon, saw that his teammate's shot would fall short. He leaped and caught the ball, then jammed it in one motion. The buzzer sounded just as it went through the net for an amazing 54-52 win. The North Carolina State Wolfpack had done the impossible.

> **Champion: North Carolina State**
> **Winning Coach:** Jim Valvano
> **Number of Schools in Tournament: 48**
> **Best Player:** Hakeem Olajuwon,
>   Houston

1984
Georgetown Hoyas
Houston Cougars
Kentucky Wildcats
Virginia Cavaliers

The 1984 Final Four featured four top-notch college centers. Unfortunately for the Cavaliers, they did not have one of them. The loss of Ralph Sampson to the pros had left them with young Olden Polynice. He was no match for Georgetown's Patrick Ewing, Houston's Hakeem Olajuwon, and Kentucky's towers of power, Sam Bowie and Mel Turpin. Although lacking a first-rate big man, Virginia had built a good defensive team in Sampson's absence. It starred Jim Miller and Othell Wilson, and it was good enough to upset Arkansas, Syracuse, and Indiana to reach the Final Four.

Kentucky's front line also included the sensational Kenny Walker, but the Wildcats were thin at the guard position.

This made Houston and Georgetown the cofavorites to win the national championship. Clyde Drexler and Larry Micheaux had left for the pros, but Alvin Franklin and Michael Young had stepped up to become reliable scorers for the Cougars. Georgetown's defense was nicknamed "Hoya Paranoia," because it came at opponents from so many different directions. Ewing was at the heart of it, along with David Wingate, Michael Jackson, Michael Graham, and Reggie Williams.

The Wildcats played the Hoyas' style of smash-mouth basketball and nearly beat them at it. Up 29-22 at the half, Kentucky had four hot shooters, and Ewing was in trouble with three fouls. In stepped Graham, the menacing enforcer, to aid Ewing under the boards. Georgetown regained its confidence and held the Wildcats to a mere three baskets in the second half to win 53-40.

The Virginia-Houston game was surprisingly close. Coach Terry Holland told his players to deny Olajuwon the ball at all costs. That often left Young open, and he scored eight baskets in a nail-biting defensive battle. The Cavaliers found themselves down by two points with less than a minute left. A stolen pass led to a game-tying layup, and the two teams went into overtime at 43-43. Houston took a 2-point lead, and Virginia fouled Young. He missed a free throw that would have iced the game, but Olajuwon blocked a pass by

Patrick Ewing and John Thompson embrace after Georgetown's 84–75 victory over Houston.

Wilson that would have led to another game-tying layup, and the Cougars advanced, 49-47.

Based on the two semifinals, everyone was expecting a defensive war between Georgetown and Houston. Both teams came out running and shooting, however, as each tried to take the other's center out of the game. John Thompson shuttled Graham and Williams into the action; each specialized in spotting openings and knifing his way to the hoop. This pair was the major difference in the first half, and the Hoyas led 40-30 at intermission.

The disheartened Cougars could not make a dent in the Georgetown lead in the second half. Instead of pulling together, they began pointing fingers and screaming at one another. Guy Lewis, whose dream of a championship had been dashed twice before, watched helplessly as his team self-destructed. Georgetown won 84-75.

> **Champion: Georgetown**
> **Winning Coach: John Thompson**
> **Number of Schools in Tournament: 48**
> **Best Player: Patrick Ewing,**
>   **Georgetown**

1985
Georgetown Hoyas
Memphis State Tigers
St. John's Redmen
Villanova Wildcats

For the first time in NCAA Tournament history, sixty-four teams were invited to play. Tiny schools like Marist, Fairleigh Dickinson, and Mississippi Valley State could now stand shoulder-to-shoulder with the giants of college basketball. The expanded field also meant that more schools with decent records—who happened to play in competitive conferences—were given bids. Although the Villanova Wildcats finished third in the Big East behind St. John's and Georgetown, they were given a bid on the strength of their 19-10 mark against very tough opponents. Rollie Massimino's team was similar to the Wolfpack squad that Jim Valvano had guided to the championship two years earlier. No starter averaged more than 15 points, and no player stood out as a star. The Wildcats won with sound, fundamental basketball.

This was also true of the other Final Four schools. Georgetown returned with the same team that had won it all a season earlier. The Hoyas were one year older and one year better. St. John's had a player that reminded everyone of Larry Bird. His name was Chris Mullin, and along with frontcourt stars Walter Berry and Bill Wennington, he helped Coach Lou Carnesecca's Redmen fashion a 31-3 record coming into the Final Four. Memphis State had one of the tournament's most feared players in 6-foot-11 senior Keith Lee. He was supported by Vincent Askew, William Bedford, and Andre Turner.

In the first semifinal, Georgetown aimed to break Mullin's 100-game streak of scoring 10 or more points. The Hoyas smothered the St. John's star, which seemed to take the heart out of the Redmen. After keeping the score close for 20 minutes, they let Georgetown run away with the game. The Hoyas forced 18 turnovers and limited Mullin to 8 points in a 77-59 victory.

The game between Villanova and Memphis State was closer but often painful to watch. The Wildcats slowed the action down to a snail's pace and outhustled the Tigers for rebounds and loose balls. A frustrated Lee began grabbing and hacking, and he fouled out with just 10 points. With the fans chanting "Boring! Boring!" Massimino's players just kept plugging away. They won the game at the foul line, where they outscored Memphis State 20-7. The final score was 52-45. Center Ed Pinckney and guard Dwayne McClain were the only players who scored in double figures.

Georgetown's domination of St. John's led many to compare the Hoyas to the great San Francisco teams of the 1950s, with Bill Russell and K.C. Jones. Some said they were as good as any UCLA team that ever took the floor. None of this made Villanova fans feel very good. Even Massimino admitted that his team would have to play a perfect game to have a chance. But there *was* that chance. The fiery coach showed his players an interesting statistic. In their humiliating loss to Georgetown, the Redmen had actually made more than half their shots; it was the turnovers that killed them. Be patient against the overly aggressive Hoyas, Massimino promised, and you will get good shots. And if you make them, you'll win.

The Wildcats began the game by sagging around Ewing and denying him the ball. Reggie Williams, David Wingate, and Michael Jackson responded by hitting their open outside shots, and Georgetown opened up a lead. The Hoyas' defense was also playing well. In all, they forced 17 turnovers. Massimino watched in agony as the mistakes piled up. When his players did hang on to the ball, however, it almost always ended up in the basket. Harold Jensen, a reserve guard, hit 5 long outside shots; Pinckney,

Dwayne McClain thrusts his fist into the air as the final buzzer sounds on Villanova's remarkable 66-64 upset of Georgetown.

McClain, and Harold Pressley combined for 14 baskets in 20 attempts; and guard Gary McLain was a perfect 3-for-3. No matter what the Hoyas did, they could not pull away from Villanova.

Late in the game, with the Wildcats trailing by two, Jensen swished an 18-footer to tie the game. A steal by Pinckney led to the go-ahead basket. When Wingate's shot from the corner was off, Villanova spread the floor and won 66-64. It took a record 78 percent shooting effort to do it, but Villanova had pulled off an upset for the ages. Even the Hoyas had to appreciate the achievement of their opponents. As the Wildcats received their trophy, the Georgetown players stood and applauded.

> **Champion: Villanova**
> **Winning Coach: Rollie Massimino**
> **Number of Schools in Tournament: 64**
> **Best Player: Ed Pinckney, Villanova**

1986
Duke Blue Devils
Kansas Jayhawks
Louisville Cardinals
LSU Tigers

The 1986 Final Four was supposed to be a coming-out party for Duke coach Mike Krzyzewski. After taking over from the popular Bill Foster in 1980–81, "Coach K" went through a series of losing seasons before his top recruits finally came together as a team. Duke starred guards Johnny Dawkins and Tommy Amaker and forward Mark Alarie. With a 35-2 record heading into the Final Four, the Blue Devils were favored to win it all.

Denny Crum had other ideas. Milt Wagner, Billy Thompson, Herbert Crook, and freshman center "Never Nervous" Pervis Ellison had already boosted Louisville to four impressive victories in the tournament, and the Cardinals were on top of their game. Kansas, coached by Larry Brown, featured Danny Manning, Calvin Thompson, Ron Kellogg, and Greg Dreiling. LSU, the tournament's "Cinderella" team, reached the Final Four on the strength of stunning upsets over Purdue, Memphis State, Georgia Tech, and Kentucky.

In the first semifinal, LSU, led by Don Redden and Ricky Blanton, continued its inexplicably good play. Crum's bewildered Cardinals, who had expected to win by a blowout, found themselves behind by eight points at the half. Louisville restored order in the second half, however, and outscored LSU 52-33. Wagner, Thompson, and Crook each shot well in the 88-77 win.

The key to success for the Blue Devils against Kansas was stopping the 6-foot-10 Manning, who played and carried himself like a pro. This they did, thanks to Alarie, who stayed glued to the sophomore forward throughout the game. Dawkins was hot for Duke, but Kellogg was hitting key shots for the Jayhawks. Kansas, ahead 65-61, blew a layup that might have won the game. The Blue Devils came back to tie the score, and with 23 seconds left, freshman Danny Ferry made a short shot to put Duke ahead. Kellogg brought the ball the other way and barreled toward the basket, hoping to draw a foul. Again, Ferry made the big play. He held his ground and drew an offensive foul. The game was Duke's, 71-67.

Both teams in the championship had 21-game winning streaks. Louisville's strategy for continuing its streak depended on limit-

Duke's Tommy Amaker gets advice from coach Mike Krzyzewski during the 1986 NCAA Final. Louisville beat the Blue Devils with a great run in the final minutes.

took the lead with less than 5 minutes left. For the first time all year, Duke failed to make big plays when it had to, and Crum had his second championship, 72-69.

> **Champion: Louisville**
> **Winning Coach: Denny Crum**
> **Number of Schools in Tournament: 64**
> **Best Player: Pervis Ellison, Louisville**

1987
Indiana Hoosiers
Providence Friars
Syracuse Orangemen
Nevada-Las Vegas Runnin' Rebels

When the 45-second shot clock and the three-pointer came to college basketball, no coach was more affected than Indiana's Bobby Knight. For years he had preached patience, and he had two national titles to show for it. Now he had to completely revamp his offensive approach. Knight also had to adjust his thinking about recruiting junior college players. These young men sometimes had academic problems, and because they had already spent a year or two playing ball elsewhere, they did not have much time to learn Knight's system. It was a combination that Knight found unappealing. Still, when the 1986–87 season opened, the Hoosiers' offense was in the hands of a couple of "juco" transfers—guard Keith Smart and center Dean Garrett. They joined guard Steve Alford, a deadly outside shooter, along with Daryl Thomas and Rick Calloway.

Jerry Tarkanian's UNLV team did not need much revamping. He had always liked the run-and-gun style, and with guard

ing the effectiveness of Dawkins. Duke aimed to keep its streak alive by shutting down Thompson and Wagner. The Blue Devils succeeded in stopping the Cardinals' two top scorers in the first half, while Louisville was unable to contain Dawkins. The Cardinals stayed close thanks to Ellison, who was enjoying the best game of his young life. Not only was he hitting shots and grabbing offensive rebounds, he was also getting the entire Duke front line into foul trouble. In the second half, Wagner increased the defensive pressure on Dawkins, and Louisville finally

Indiana's Joe Hillman strips the ball from Syracuse star Sherman Douglas. The Hoosiers made several big plays in their rousing 74–73 victory.

Mark Wade feeding scorers Armand Gilliam and Freddie Banks, the Runnin' Rebels did not worry much about the shot clock. The surprise of the tournament was Providence, which rained down three-pointers on heavily favored Alabama and Georgetown to reach the Final Four. Much of the credit for the Friars' success went to coach Rick Pitino, a superb strategist and master motivator. Syracuse, led by power forward Derrick Coleman, center Ron Seikaly, and guard Sherman Douglas, was given an even chance along with Indiana to win it all.

In the first semifinal, Knight decided to ambush Tarkanian by outrunning the Rebels. Racing downcourt before UNLV could set up, Hoosier ball handlers drew two defenders and then kicked the ball out to Alford, who either canned long jumpers or drew fouls with drives of his own. Banks and Gilliam heated up in the second half, and the game went right down to the wire. A pair of offensive foul calls against UNLV gave Indiana an opportunity to pull away, and Knight's troops did just that. The Hoosiers won, 97-93.

The second game failed to produce the same excitement. Providence three-point specialists Billy Donovan and Delray Brooks were ice-cold, and the Orangemen beat the Friars to almost every loose ball. The final score was 77-63, Syracuse.

The championship game was exciting from start to finish. Alford and Smart got Indiana off to a strong start, but Knight benched Smart after he made a stupid pass. Sensing an opportunity, Douglas began driving to the hoop whenever possible. When Garrett moved to stop him, the Syracuse point guard simply dished off to Seikaly for easy baskets. The Orangemen put together a 14-3 run be-

fore Smart was reinserted and shut down Douglas. The score at the half was 34-33, Hoosiers. The Syracuse fast break got rolling in the second half, thanks to Coleman's strong rebounds and outlet passes. This gave the Orangemen a 61-56 lead with less than 8 minutes left. Once again, Smart came to the rescue. He made several clutch shots down the stretch and brought Indiana to within a point, 73-72, with about 30 seconds left.

Coleman received the inbound pass and was immediately fouled. He missed his free throw, and Indiana got the ball back with a chance to win. Knight called a play that would free Alford (who already had 7 three-pointers) for a jumper, but Syracuse had him covered. With time running out, Smart had the ball near the left baseline. He rose in the air and flicked a soft 15-footer toward the basket. It swished through the net as the buzzer sounded for a heart-stopping 74-73 win.

Champion: Indiana
Winning Coach: Bobby Knight
Number of Schools in Tournament: 64
Best Player: Keith Smart, Indiana

1988
Arizona Wildcats
Duke Blue Devils
Kansas Jayhawks
Oklahoma Sooners

Thirty years had passed since a Big Eight Conference team won a game in the Final Four. So when Billy Tubbs's Oklahoma Sooners reached the Big Dance, no one expected much. That was a mistake. As their 33-3 record showed, the Sooners had an

Oklahoma's Stacey King watches helplessly as Danny Manning throws one down in Kansas's 83–79 win.

excellent team. Stacey King and Horace Grant were two of the best frontcourt players in the country, and Mookie Blaylock was an awesome guard. Many of their victories were blowouts.

Kansas, Duke, and Arizona, however, were every bit Oklahoma's equal. Danny Manning had become a superstar for the Jayhawks, who surrounded him with a solid supporting cast, including Milt Newton and Kevin Pritchard. Duke's Danny Ferry had

become a big star, too. He led a deep Blue Devils team that was 28-6 heading into the Final Four. Arizona, with Sean Elliott, Steve Kerr, and Tom Tolbert, also had the talent to go all the way.

Kansas made quick work of Duke in the first semifinal. With Newton firing three-pointers and the Jayhawks' defense shutting down the Blue Devils' attack, Larry Brown's squad built an insurmountable 24-6 lead. Duke did attempt a second-half comeback, but when the Blue Devils got close, Manning—who finished with 25 points, 10 rebounds, and 6 blocked shots—took over and put the game away, 66-59.

Arizona hoped to attack Oklahoma early, too. But Coach Tubbs had an ingenious plan. Figuring that Elliott would get his 30 points no matter what, he told his players to concentrate on the other Wildcats—especially the three-point-shooting Kerr. Blaylock limited Kerr to 6 points; Elliott scored 31; Grant played well inside; and the Sooners won, 86-78.

Oklahoma was licking its chops for a shot at Kansas. The two schools had played twice during the year, and the Sooners had won both times. Tubbs prevailed in contests by sending waves of defenders at Manning, and he saw no reason to change his strategy. Coach Brown told his players to be patient, that the Sooners would start to tire if they did not grab the momentum immediately. Kansas got the early advantage when its guards began hitting long jumpers. This stretched the defense and gave Manning more room to maneuver inside. On the other end, the Sooners were hitting their shots. At halftime the score was deadlocked at 50-50.

Normally, Oklahoma would have opened the second half with an aggressive full-court press. But the Sooners' guards, Blaylock and Ricky Grace, were both in foul trouble. Fearing the loss of his floor generals, Tubbs abandoned his usual up-tempo style and tried to beat Kansas at its own half-court game. Now the Jayhawks could feed Manning whenever they pleased. The junior hit 13 shots, grabbed 18 rebounds, and sank the free throws that put the game out of reach. Kansas won, 83-79.

> **Champion: Kansas**
> **Winning Coach: Larry Brown**
> **Number of Schools in Tournament: 64**
> **Best Player: Danny Manning, Kansas**

1989
Duke Blue Devils
Illinois Fighting Illini
Michigan Wolverines
Seton Hall Pirates

Every few years, a "Cinderella" team gets into the Final Four—a school that, at the beginning of the year, did not think it had a shot at the NCAA crown. In 1989, there were two "Cinderella" coaches. Steve Fisher, an assistant to Bill Frieder at Michigan during the 1988–89 season, was promoted to head coach a few days before the tournament. Frieder had accepted a job at Arizona State for the following year, and in an unusual move, angry school officials had thrown him out. P.J. Carlesimo brought his Seton Hall team to the tournament a year after students at the New Jersey school had mounted a campaign to have him fired. It is safe to say that neither man dreamed he would be standing within two wins of a national championship in the spring of 1989.

Michigan had an excellent team that starred sharpshooter Glen Rice, floor leader Rumeal Robinson, forward Terry Mills, and rebounding demon Loy Vaught. Seton Hall featured the meteoric John Morton, hulking Ramon Ramos, and Australian star Andrew Gaze. The Final Four favorites, however, were Illinois and Duke. The Illini were paced by the sensational duo of Nick Anderson and Kendall Gill, both of whom could score from any spot on the floor.

Michigan players stream on to the floor after Rumeal Robinson's free throws win the game. The NCAA Final featured two "Cinderella" teams, and the game was decided in overtime.

Duke had added freshman center Christian Laettner to an already powerful squad that included Danny Ferry, Robert Brickey, and Phil Henderson.

The glass slipper fit perfectly in the semifinals, as both Michigan and Seton Hall prevailed. The Wolverines eked out an 83-81 win over Illinois on a three-point play by reserve Mark Hughes and a put-back shot by another bench player, Sean Higgins.

Seton Hall looked dead after allowing Duke to roll up a 26-8 lead, but by halftime the Pirates had gotten the score back to 38-33. The game remained tight until Laettner was benched with foul trouble. The Pirates worked the ball inside, made their shots, and slowly pulled away to a 95-78 victory.

Michigan, playing relaxed and confident ball, sprinted out to an early lead in the final. Rice was on fire, while Gaze and Morton could not buy a hoop for the Pirates. Seton Hall pulled together and closed the gap to 37-32 by halftime. Still, Michigan felt it was on the verge of blowing the game open. Morton put an end to those thoughts when he scored 17 points in the final 8 minutes. His last basket was a three-pointer that sent the game into overtime.

With Seton Hall ahead in the extra period, Morton suddenly lost his touch and missed a key shot. The Wolverines came roaring back to cut the Pirates' lead to a single point. With time running out, Robinson got the ball for Michigan, put his head down, and drove to the hoop. The referee whistled Seton Hall for a foul, and the sophomore guard—a lousy free-throw shooter—calmly hit both shots for an 81-80 win. It was a rags-to-riches story that Cinderella herself might not have believed. Coach Fisher, who did not win a game during the regular season, had won it all.

Champion: Michigan
Winning Coach: Steve Fisher
Number of Schools in Tournament: 64
Best Player: Glen Rice, Michigan

CHAPTER 6

THE 1990s

1990
Arkansas Razorbacks
Duke Blue Devils
Georgia Tech Yellow Jackets
Nevada-Las Vegas Runnin' Rebels

The NCAA Tournament officially became big business in 1990, when the CBS television network paid $1 billion for the rights to broadcast it. In past years, the early-round action had been televised quite expertly by ESPN. Now the pressure was on CBS to give fans the same kind of coverage. As luck would have it, the 1990 tournament really was "March Madness" (a phrase coined in the 1980s), as each round was marked by wild, buzzer-beating finishes and major upsets. Put to the test, CBS came through with flying colors.

Four excellent teams survived the insanity to reach the Final Four. Arkansas boasted a deep, well-balanced team led by Todd Day, Len Howell, and Lee Mayberry. Georgia Tech had the best guard in the tournament—Kenny Anderson—along with the best pure shooter, Dennis Scott. Duke was led by freshman point guard Bobby Hurley and a front line of Christian Laettner, Alaa Abdelnaby, and Phil Henderson. The team to beat was UNLV, which had the country's top

all-around player in Larry Johnson. "LJ" had a great supporting cast, including Anderson Hunt, Greg Anthony, and Stacey Augmon.

With three players averaging 20 points a game, the Yellow Jackets were the only team with a chance to outgun UNLV. In a thrilling semifinal, they got terrific performances from Anderson, Scott, and Brian Oliver. After Georgia Tech took a 53-46 lead into halftime, Jerry Tarkanian decided to switch from a loose zone to an aggressive man-to-man defense. In the time it took the Yellow Jackets to adjust, the Rebels went on a 10-1 run to grab the lead. Augmon stepped up at this point and made big plays at both ends of the floor, allowing UNLV to pull away for a 90-81 win.

Arkansas coach Nolan Richardson liked to overwhelm opponents with wave after wave of fresh defenders, but there was little he could do against Laettner and Abdelnaby. The Duke big men killed Arkansas in the paint. Day kept the Razorbacks in the game with 27 points, but the Blue Devils simply overpowered them, 97-83.

Duke had to play a near-perfect game to beat UNLV in the NCAA Final. Although the two teams matched up well on paper, if the Blue Devils did not hit their shots, the Rebels' running game would blow them off

Moses Scurry grabs one of his six rebounds against Duke in the 1990 NCAA Final. The UNLV Runnin' Rebels became the first team to eclipse the century mark in a championship game with their 103-73 blowout of the Blue Devils.

the court. From the opening tip-off, Hunt and Anthony made life miserable for Hurley (who was suffering from the flu), and the Duke offense stalled. Johnson, meanwhile, was too much to handle inside. Duke fans felt lucky to make it to halftime down by only 12 points. This feeling was confirmed in the opening minutes of the second half, when UNLV ran wild and scored 18 points in 3 minutes. The Rebels kept

pouring it on and won 103-73—the first time a national champion had cracked the 100-point barrier.

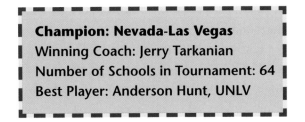

Champion: Nevada-Las Vegas
Winning Coach: Jerry Tarkanian
Number of Schools in Tournament: 64
Best Player: Anderson Hunt, UNLV

1991

Duke Blue Devils
Kansas Jayhawks
North Carolina Tar Heels
Nevada-Las Vegas Runnin' Rebels

Another strong field made up the 1991 Final Four, but all eyes were on the semifinal meeting between Duke and UNLV. Mike Krzyzewski and the Blue Devils were still stinging from the beating suffered at the hands of the Runnin' Rebels in the 1990 championship game. UNLV was 34-0 heading into the Final Four. Larry Johnson looked like a man among boys, while Anderson Hunt, Stacey Augmon, and Greg Anthony had all moved their games up a notch. Duke, at 30-7, had the deepest, youngest, most consistent team in the country. Christian Laettner and Bobby Hurley were complemented by freshman Grant Hill and sophomores Billy McCaffrey and Thomas Hill. The only senior on the roster was reserve forward Greg Koubek.

The winner of the Duke-UNLV game would play either Kansas or North Carolina. Mark Randall and his fellow Jayhawks gave coach Roy Williams a consistent, workmanlike effort every night. The Tar Heels were led by George Lynch, Rick Fox, Eric Montross, and Hubert Davis. They too had a deep bench, but unlike his Duke counterpart, coach Dean Smith never knew what kind of performances he would get from one game to the next. Often he was forced to make dozens of substitutions before finding the right on-floor chemistry.

Unfortunately for Smith, the semifinal against Kansas was one of those games. He made a staggering number of substitutions—93 in all—and found himself playing from behind right from the start. Randall and Adonis Jordan led the Jayhawks to a 79-73 victory. The game ended with Kansas coach Roy Williams (an assistant to Smith for 10 years) using Carolina's famous four-corner stall.

In the Duke-UNLV matchup, Coach Krzyzewski decided to go man-to-man, with Laettner helping out on Johnson whenever he came into the paint. Grant Hill and junior Brian Davis concentrated on stopping Augmon. On offense, Hurley forced Anthony to chase him all over the court, and the Rebels' point guard began picking up cheap fouls. Many UNLV players had predicted that the game would be over in 10 minutes, but after 20 minutes Duke was hanging tough at 43-41. As the game entered its final 10 minutes, Duke clearly had no intention of fading away.

Sensing the mounting pressure on the Rebels, the Blue Devils decided to send a message. Hunt, the MVP of the 1990 Final Four, got the ball with a clear path to the basket. Rather than allowing him to dunk, the diminutive Hurley smashed into him in midair, preventing the basket. Inspired by their floor leader, other Duke players got into the act. They began throwing their weight around on rebounds and giving up their bodies to draw charging calls. The turning point of the game was the offensive foul that Brian Davis created by letting Anthony plow into him on a layup. On this play, UNLV could have gone ahead 77-71 with under 4 minutes left. Instead, their lead stayed at 74-71. More importantly, Anthony was now on the bench with five fouls. This gave the Blue Devils an advantage because Hunt, the Rebels' best outside shooter, was forced to play point guard. Duke tied the score and then went ahead 79-77 on free throws by Laettner. Twelve seconds later, Hunt's panicked shot at the buzzer missed badly, and Duke had its sweet revenge.

Fearful of an emotional letdown in the NCAA Final, Krzyzewski reminded his players that there was still one game to play. Laettner was exhausted, which meant that players like McCaffrey and Grant Hill would have to step up with points and rebounds. And Hurley had to be great again. Two minutes into the game, Hill energized the Blue Devils with one of the greatest dunks ever caught on film. Rising to the hoop for an alley-oop, the freshman saw the pass floating behind him instead of in front

of him. He arched and twisted in midair, caught the ball in one hand, then jackknifed forward to slam the ball through the basket. The Blue Devils built an 8-point halftime lead, as the Jayhawks missed several easy shots in the early going, and only Randall seemed to be playing his game. Kansas failed to pick things up in the second half, and Duke began to pull away. McCaffrey was scoring, Hill was rebounding, Hurley was running the offense well, and Laettner was hitting his foul shots. The final score was 72-65, but the Jayhawks never threatened seriously.

Champion: Duke
Winning Coach: Mike Krzyzewski
Number of Schools in Tournament: 64
Best Player: Christian Laettner, Duke

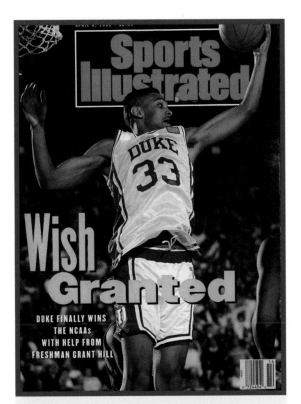

Duke found its long-awaited "missing ingredient" in freshman Grant Hill. It was he, not Christian Laettner, who graced *Sports Illustrated*'s cover after the title game.

1992

Cincinnati Bearcats
Duke Blue Devils
Indiana Hoosiers
Michigan Wolverines

For 10 years, Duke coach Mike Krzyzewski had to listen to reasons why he could not bring a championship to the school. With that monkey off his back, he now looked to make it two NCAA titles. The Blue Devils were a powerhouse, with Christian Laettner, Bobby Hurley, Grant Hill, and a terrific supporting cast. Sophomore forward Antonio Lang was now an important contributor, as was freshman center Cherokee Parks. Ironically, Duke almost did not make it to the Final Four—it took a last-second 104-103 win over Kentucky in the Regional Final.

After that, Bobby Knight, who once

SO LONG, STRETCH

For nearly 50 years, the NCAA Tournament was a showcase for the best college centers. Most conferences had at least one big man whom they felt was the equal of anyone in the country, and the tournament was the place they could prove it. When these titans clashed in a Final Four match, it made the comparisons all the more thrilling. In the 1980s, two rules were adopted by the NCAA Tournament in order to make the games more exciting: the 45-second shot clock (later reduced to 35 seconds) and the three-point shot.

No one realized it at the time, but these rules would drastically limit the role of the college center. With offenses pressured to take quick shots, there was not always time to work the ball into the low post, especially when the center was surrounded by zone defenders. Knowing this, centers began spending more time setting screens and getting ready for rebounds than they did fighting to get in to scoring position. The three-point line had a similar effect on centers. With the line ridiculously close to the basket, it was much safer to take open jumpers from 20 feet than to force passes into the lane. Also, when ball handlers penetrated into the middle, they were just as likely to kick the ball back to the perimeter than to make a pass in traffic to a fumble-fingered center.

Will we see the return of the classic center to college basketball someday? Sadly, the answer is probably no.

coached Krzyzewski as a player, figured to be the Blue Devils' main roadblock on the way to the championship. His Hoosiers were led by Calbert Cheaney, Damon Bailey, Greg Graham, and Alan Henderson. Cincinnati's Bearcats, starring guard Nick Van Exel, reached the Final Four partly in thanks to early-round losses by Kansas and Southern California. The most interesting school in the Final Four had to be Michigan. Steve Fisher's Wolverines included five freshmen who, by midseason, had completely taken over. He decided to let the kids play, believing that it would help them in future seasons. He was as surprised as any-

one when the "Fab Five"—Chris Webber, Jalen Rose, Juwan Howard, Jimmy King, and Ray Jackson—made it past Oklahoma State and Ohio State to reach the Final Four.

Each winning team in the semifinals trailed at the half. Indiana led Duke 42-37 at intermission, with both schools shooting well. The difference in this game was not points but fouls. Four Hoosiers found themselves in foul trouble early in the second half, and Duke pressed its advantage to open up a comfortable lead. In the closing minutes, a barrage of Indiana three-pointers made the game close, but the Blue Devils prevailed, 81-78.

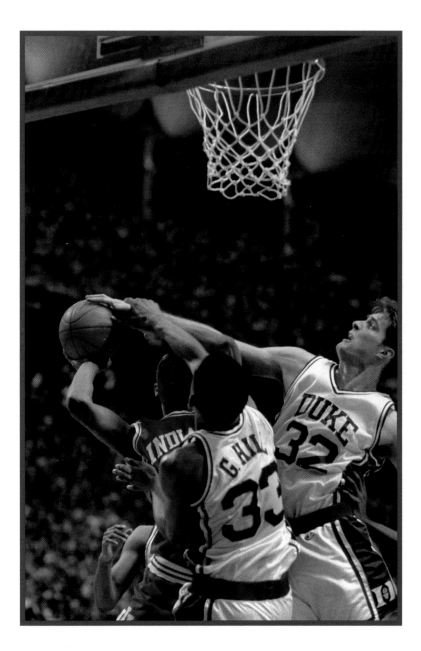

Grant Hill and Christian Laettner team up to stuff Indiana's Alan Henderson in the national semifinal. Duke won 81–78 to advance.

The Bearcats led their game against Michigan 41-38 after the first 20 minutes. Van Exel had the hot hand for Cincinnati, but he cooled off in the second half. Howard, Webber, and Rose began to work for shots closer to the basket, and Michigan went ahead. King made several clutch baskets down the stretch for the Wolverines, who won 76-72.

The final was a battle of youth versus experience. The Duke starters had played for all the marbles in 1991—at about the same time the Michigan starters were getting ready for their high-school proms. At the beginning of the game, the young Wolverines swarmed all over the Blue Devils. Laettner was having ballhandling problems, and his teammates seemed a step slower than their enthusiastic opponents. At halftime, the score was 31-30, Michigan.

In the locker room, Krzyzewski and Hurley made passionate speeches, and the Blue Devils returned to the floor looking like champions. They shut down the cocky, overconfident Wolverines, who scored just 21 points the rest of the way. The game remained fairly close until Duke went on an 8-0 run with 7 minutes left. At that point Michigan just gave up. The final score was 71-51.

Champion: Duke
Winning Coach: Mike Krzyzewski
Number of Schools in Tournament: 64
Best Player: Bobby Hurley, Duke

1993
Kansas Jayhawks
Kentucky Wildcats
Michigan Wolverines
North Carolina Tar Heels

With Mike Krzyzewski getting all the headlines in the Atlantic Coast Conference, the basketball world tended to forget that there was another terrific coach just a few miles down the road in Chapel Hill. His name was Dean Smith, and he had guided his North Carolina teams—some good, some not so good—to the NCAA Tournament for a remarkable 21 years in a row. Unlike his counterpart in Durham, however, Smith was still waiting for that elusive second championship. Smith's 1992–93 squad did not seem likely to deliver. Eric Montross and George Lynch were good rebounders, and guard Derrick Phelps was a capable playmaker, but no

one had established himself as a consistent clutch scorer during the year. The Tar Heels reached the Final Four thanks to a tight defense and to the surprising shooting of sophomore guard Donald Williams. Could Williams keep it up?

Roy Williams did not think so. His Jayhawks, led by Adonis Jordan and Rex Walters, were already looking across the draw at the tournament favorite, Michigan. Steve Fisher's "Fab Five" were even more fabulous as sophomores. Chris Webber and Juwan Howard gave the Wolverines a great front line, while Jalen Rose created tremendous matchup problems with his size and ballhandling ability. The Kentucky Wildcats, led by Jamal Mashburn and coached by Rick Pitino, were eager to prove that the previous year's loss to Duke had been just a bump in the road on their way to a national championship.

From the opening moments of the UNC-Kansas semifinal, it was clear that Coach Williams had underestimated the Tar Heels' ability to score from the perimeter. With Montross and Lynch occupying defenders close to the basket, the floor opened up for the Carolina jump-shooters. Williams started the game on fire, hitting several long bombs. Walters and Jordan kept pace for the Jayhawks, and the game remained close right to the end. With less than 3 minutes left, Williams hit his fifth three-pointer of the game, and Carolina pulled away for a 78-68 win.

Michigan and Kentucky played an even closer semifinal. The run-and-gun Wildcats gave the Wolverines a ton of trouble, with Mashburn scoring 26 points on powerful drives and pull-up jumpers. Michigan hung close by feeding the ball to Webber, who scored 29 against Kentucky's pint-sized

George Lynch of the Tar Heels puts a little extra mustard on this dunk against the Michigan Wolverines. UNC won a close game in the final moments.

frontcourt players. The Wildcats appeared to gain an advantage after Webber fouled out in overtime, but Rose and Howard picked up the slack and the Wolverines triumphed, 81-78.

The Tar Heels entered the NCAA Final as a slight underdog, but Coach Smith had plotted a strategy that he believed would keep his team in the game. He designed a zone defense that limited Michigan's inside play and told his players to work for good shots on offense. Once again, Williams stepped up and began hitting clutch baskets from long range, and Carolina built a 42-36 halftime lead.

Coach Fisher countered Smith's defense in the second half by freeing up guard Jimmy King for medium-range jump shots. Michigan clawed its way back, then moved ahead by 4 points with 6 minutes left. Coach Smith called time and urged his starters to show the country what a disciplined, experienced team could do down the stretch. They responded by regaining the lead, 73-71. With less than a minute left, the Wolverines were forced to foul and hope for the best.

When Carolina missed its free throw, Webber grabbed the rebound and turned upcourt. Neither guard came back to help him, so the 6-foot-10 forward decided to dribble it himself. The Tar Heels forced him into the right corner and set up a trap. Recognizing he was in trouble, Webber instinctively signalled for a time-out. But Michigan had already used its last time-out, and Webber was whistled for a technical foul. Carolina got two free throws plus possession of the ball. With 11 seconds left, there was nothing the crestfallen Webber could do but watch the Tar Heels win 77-71.

> **Champion: North Carolina**
> **Winning Coach: Dean Smith**
> **Number of Schools in Tournament: 64**
> **Best Player: Donald Williams,**
> **North Carolina**

1994
Arizona Wildcats
Arkansas Razorbacks
Duke Blue Devils
Florida Gators

The 1994 Final Four was tough to figure. With a quartet of good teams—each with multiple go-to guys and each well-coached—no one could predict the outcome with any confidence. Duke was the favorite, mostly because the Blue Devils had won twice before. Grant Hill was in his final season, and he captained a team that included Cherokee Parks, Antonio Lang, and Jeff Capel. Florida, led by Andrew DeClercq and coached by Lon Kruger, was the surprise team in the tournament. The Gators had reached the Final Four by upsetting UConn and then defeating Boston College, which had scored a couple of major upsets itself. Arizona relied on three good guards— Khalid Reeves, Damon Stoudamire, and Reggie Geary—and wily Lute Olson, who had coached the team to 29 victories. Arkansas, under Nolan Richardson, had both the defense and the depth to win. It also had a couple of special players in Corliss Williamson and Scotty Thurman. Both had proved capable of rising to the challenge of big games.

Against Arizona, the Razorbacks got a huge performance from Williamson, who killed the Wildcats with his inside play. The sophomore forward scored 29 points, while Arizona's guards never found their shooting touch. This proved the difference in a 91-82 victory for the Razorbacks.

Duke won its semifinal, but not without a scare. The Gators matched up well with the Blue Devils and played with great intensity. At halftime, Florida was up 39-32. Led by Hill, Duke eventually grabbed a 66-65 lead. With 14 seconds left, Parks followed his own miss with a short basket to put the Blue Devils up by three. On the other end, Lang drew an offensive foul and made his free throws to put the game away, 70-65.

Duke's starting five was better than Arkansas's, but the Razorback bench was deeper. Coach Richardson knew he had to put that bench into play or Mike Krzyzewski would win a third NCAA title. In the first half, the Blue Devils handled Richardson's pressing defense with ease. Parks and Lang played well inside and converted key baskets after the Duke guards managed to shake loose from their pursuers. Only a strong performance from guard Corey Beck enabled the Razorbacks to keep pace. Arkansas's defensive frenzy continued in the second half, but again the Blue Devils handled it with ease. At one point, Duke was ahead by 10. Perhaps sensing that the game was in hand, the Blue Devils relaxed for a moment. This was a mistake, for when Williamson and Thurman led an Arkansas comeback, Krzyzewski's players were unable to find their second wind.

Richardson's substitution strategy was finally paying off, and he now had the fresher players. The Razorbacks stormed ahead, 70-67. Hill, who had been kept in check all game, hit a three-pointer for the Blue Devils to tie the score. Arkansas worked patiently on their next possession to

The close-knit Razorbacks share a moment before hitting the floor against Duke. Arkansas beat Duke 76–72 on a clutch shot by Scotty Thurman.

get a good shot, but Duke's defense clamped down. With one second remaining on the shot clock—and less than a minute left in the game—Thurman launched a rainbow with a Blue Devil defender in his face. Somehow it settled into the basket, and the Razorbacks held on for a 76-72 win.

1995
Arkansas Razorbacks
North Carolina Tar Heels
Oklahoma State Cowboys
UCLA Bruins

Had it really been 20 years since the UCLA Bruins stood atop the college basketball world? Indeed it had. Although the school had produced fine players in the 1980s and early 1990s—including Reggie Miller, Pooh Richardson, Stuart Gray, Tracy Murray, Don MacLean, and Mark Eaton—they never had the right mix to get past the tournament's first few rounds. In 1988–89, UCLA hired Jim Harrick to coach the Bruins, and things began to change. In 1992, his team won 25 times during the season and was awarded a number-one seed in the tournament, but the Bruins lost in the Regional Final to Indiana. In 1995, Harrick finally had all the pieces. The O'Bannon brothers—Ed and Charles—led a squad that featured guards Tyus Edney and Toby Bailey. Edney had been a one-man highlight show in the early rounds, driving through traffic and sinking one unbelievable shot after another. His end-to-end layup in the second round to beat Missouri at the buzzer is still one of the tournament's most famous moments.

UCLA's mission was to unseat one of the two previous champions, who waited on the other side of the draw. The Razorbacks

still had Corliss Williamson and Scotty Thurman, while Dean Smith's Tar Heels boasted young superstars Jerry Stackhouse and Rasheed Wallace. First Harrick had to slip past Eddie Sutton's Oklahoma State team, whose big man—Bryant "Big Country" Reeves—was having a heck of a tournament himself.

Without a star center, the Bruins watched helplessly as Reeves continued his hot shooting. Making matters worse for UCLA was the fact that Ed O'Bannon, their best player, was off his game. Ed's brother teamed with Edney to pick up the slack, and the Bruins fought their way to a 37-37 half-

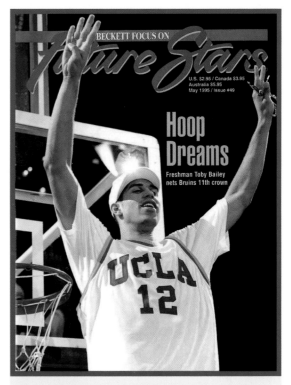

Toby Bailey never did become a big star, but the freshman played the game of his life against Arkansas in the 1995 NCAA Final.

time tie. Reeves cooled off in the second half, and this enabled UCLA to go on an 11-0 run. The Cowboys mounted a comeback charge but never caught up. The final score was 75-68.

The UNC-Arkansas game was a wild affair that saw both teams bombing away from three-point territory in a close first half. In the second half, Nolan Richardson ordered the ball inside to Williamson, who scored 19 points in 20 minutes to give the Razorbacks a big lead. The Tar Heels fought back in the final minutes, but Arkansas guard Clint McDaniel made 4 important free throws to put the game away, 71-68.

Although UCLA was a slight underdog in the final, few believed that the famous Arkansas press would work against Edney. Once he began penetrating, the Razorbacks' defense would be shredded apart. Three minutes into the game, Bruins fans gasped as Edney went down hard and had to leave the game with a badly sprained wrist. Backup Cameron Dollar, who averaged less than four points a game, took Edney's place. Although understandably nervous, Dollar held his own against the pressing Razorbacks. Meanwhile, Ed O'Bannon was winning his head-to-head battle against Williamson. The Bruins went into intermission ahead, 40-39.

Dollar continued his good play in the second half, as did O'Bannon, who finished with 30 points and 17 rebounds. Arkansas began to double-team these two, which left Bailey wide open. The enthusiastic freshman began popping short jumpers and even driving the lane, and quite suddenly the Razorbacks found themselves down by 11 points. With Williamson and Thurman shooting poorly, Richardson looked to his

bench players for help. Led by Al Dillard and Lee Wilson, they responded brilliantly and cut the deficit to 69-65. But UCLA regained its composure thanks to a clutch tip-in by Bailey, and the Razorbacks never got any closer. A generation after their last NCAA title, the Bruins were champions again, 89-78.

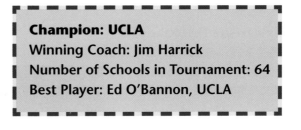

Champion: UCLA
Winning Coach: Jim Harrick
Number of Schools in Tournament: 64
Best Player: Ed O'Bannon, UCLA

1996
Kentucky Wildcats
Massachusetts Minutemen
Mississippi State Bulldogs
Syracuse Orangemen

Rick Pitino and the Wildcats were back in the Final Four with a deep, talented squad that specialized in "racehorse" basketball. Kentucky ran wire-to-wire; if you couldn't keep up, you lost. This was the challenge facing the other three schools, each of which felt it had an answer to Pitino's breakneck pace. UMass, the top-ranked team in the country, had a center who could run the floor as well as most guards. His name was Marcus Camby, and he was the centerpiece of an otherwise ordinary squad that John Calipari had coached to 35 wins. The tournament's two surprise teams—Mississippi State and Syracuse—had relied on star players all year, too. The Bulldogs' Dontae Jones was a deadly open-court player, while John Wallace gave the Orangemen a scorer and rebounder who could be effective in any scheme coach Jim

Boeheim concocted. The Wildcats, how-ever, were loaded. They had Tony Delk, An-toine Walker, Walter McCarty, Ron Mercer, and Derek Anderson—any one of whom could score 20 points in a game.

Because Kentucky and UMass met in the semifinals, their game got the bulk of the attention. Few fans doubted that the winner of this game would roll over

whichever school emerged from the other side of the draw. As expected, the Wildcats came out running, and the Minutemen kept pace. The difference was the freshman Mer-cer, who was playing particularly well at both ends of the court. With his normally hot-shooting guards—Edgar Padilla and Carmello Travieso—missing their shots, Calipari used every trick in the book to stay

Kentucky's Walter McCarty chats with an official during the national semi-final. The Wildcats beat UMass to earn a trip to the NCAA Final.

close to Kentucky. Midway through the second half, the Wildcats managed to carve out an 8-point lead. From there, Walker and Delk took over and the Minutemen were eliminated, 81-74.

In the other Final Four tilt, Syracuse got unexpectedly good shooting performances from Todd Burgan and Otis Hill. This gave Wallace more room to operate, and he burned the Bulldogs again and again. Although Jones, Erick Dampier, and Daryl Wilson kept Mississippi State close for 20 minutes, the game slipped away in the second half. Syracuse won, 77-69.

Pitino and Boeheim were happy to face each other in the final. Pitino's first major break in the coaching business had come 20 years earlier, when Boeheim hired him as an assistant. The two had remained friends, and now one would win his first NCAA title. Boeheim planned to slow Kentucky's game down with his zone defense, which was one of the best in the country. Expecting this, Pitino told his players to take three-point shots to "spread the floor" and to create wider lanes to the basket. Wallace and Burgan started strong for the Orangemen, while the Wildcats struggled to find out who had the hot hand. Eventually, Delk and Mercer began hitting shots, and Kentucky grabbed a 9-point lead at the half.

Syracuse shaved 7 points off the deficit early in the second half, but Boeheim's troops were getting tired. He watched in frustration as Kentucky's fresh reserves kept up the pressure, and as his Orangemen lost the ball on their next six possessions. After Delk hit his seventh three-pointer of the game, the Wildcats went on to win, 76-67. In the end, Kentucky's depth had been the difference. Pitino's bench outscored Boeheim's 26-0.

> **Champion: Kentucky**
> **Winning Coach: Rick Pitino**
> **Number of Schools in Tournament: 64**
> **Best Player: Tony Delk, Kentucky**

1997
Arizona Wildcats
Kentucky Wildcats
Minnesota Gophers
North Carolina Tar Heels

Once again, Kentucky had the team to beat in the NCAA Tournament. Although Tony Delk, Antoine Walker, Walter McCarty, and Derek Anderson had moved on to the NBA, Rick Pitino still had incredible depth. In fact, Wildcats had so much talent that senior Jeff Sheppard sat out the season as a redshirt for fear that he might not play. Sophomore Ron Mercer was now the top cat in Kentucky, along with fellow guard Anthony Epps.

Lute Olson had his Arizona Wildcats back in the Final Four for the third time. The team was led by a trio of unguardable guards—Miles Simon, Mike Bibby, and Jason Terry—along with forward Michael Dickerson. Dean Smith, in what would be his final season, was counting on Antawn Jamison and Vince Carter to deliver a third NCAA title. Minnesota, coached by Clem Haskins, had a well-balanced squad led by guard Bobby Jackson. The Gophers had eliminated UCLA to reach their first ever Final Four.

The Tar Heels looked like certain finalists when they sprinted out to a 15-4 advantage over Arizona, but Simon and Bibby caught fire and led a charge that had the Wildcats leading at the half by a score of

Miles Simon leans in for a layup during Arizona's overtime win against Kentucky.

34-31. Carolina looked for more production from guard Shammond Williams in the second half, but he threw up one brick after another. In no time, Arizona had a 15-point lead. Smith's troops rallied to make the game close, but a three-pointer by Bibby with 2 minutes left broke their spirit, and Arizona took the game, 66-58.

In its semifinal against Minnesota, Kentucky also built a big lead only to see it evaporate. Mercer and Epps converted a flurry of Gopher turnovers into a comfortable halftime lead, but in the second half Jackson sparked a 9-0 run that put Minnesota in front. Trailing 52-51, Pitino's players rallied to outscore the Gophers 17-5. The Wildcats coasted from there to win, 78-69.

Fans expecting a close, high-scoring game between the Wildcats and Wildcats were not disappointed by the 1997 NCAA final. Olson's strategy was to keep the pressure on Kentucky with Simon and Bibby and to shut down the high-scoring Mercer. Knowing his star would get extra attention, Pitino told guard Wayne Turner to look for more scoring opportunities. As always, Kentucky would go to the man who had the hot hand. In the early action, each team stuck to its game plan. Pitino got important points from reserves Nazr Mohammed and Cameron Mills, while Olson's players were drawing fouls whenever they ventured into the lane. With the halftime score 33-32, Arizona, it seemed that Kentucky's foul situation would be crucial as the minutes melted away.

The lead seesawed in the second half, as Epps, Turner, and Scott Padgett made big shots for Kentucky. Arizona countered with a three-guard offense. With Terry distributing the ball, Simon and Bibby were free to fire away. Kentucky fell behind, but with 12 seconds left, Epps made a clutch bucket to send the game into overtime. Once again the Arizona guards came through. Pressing the action, they drew three fouls early in the 5-minute period and made 5 quick free throws. Forced to continue fouling, Kentucky lost Mercer, Padgett, and big man Jared Prickett. Arizona made its shots to win 84-79.

Champion: Arizona
Winning Coach: Lute Olson
Number of Schools in Tournament: 64
Best Player: Miles Simon, Arizona

1998
Kentucky Wildcats
North Carolina Tar Heels
Stanford Cardinal
Utah Utes

Rick Pitino shocked Kentucky fans after the 1997 Final Four, when he announced that he would take the head coaching job with the NBA's Boston Celtics. After rebuilding the Kentucky program in the 1990s, it was time for him to take on a new challenge: restoring the NBA's most heralded franchise to its past glory. The Wildcats' new coach, Tubby Smith, found himself in an interesting situation. Kentucky had come a long way since the days when it was the center of "white basketball." Still, it had never hired a black coach before Smith. He was inheriting a team that had come within a couple of shots of winning a second straight championship. Smith sensed that there were still those who were quietly hoping he would fail. He also knew that nothing

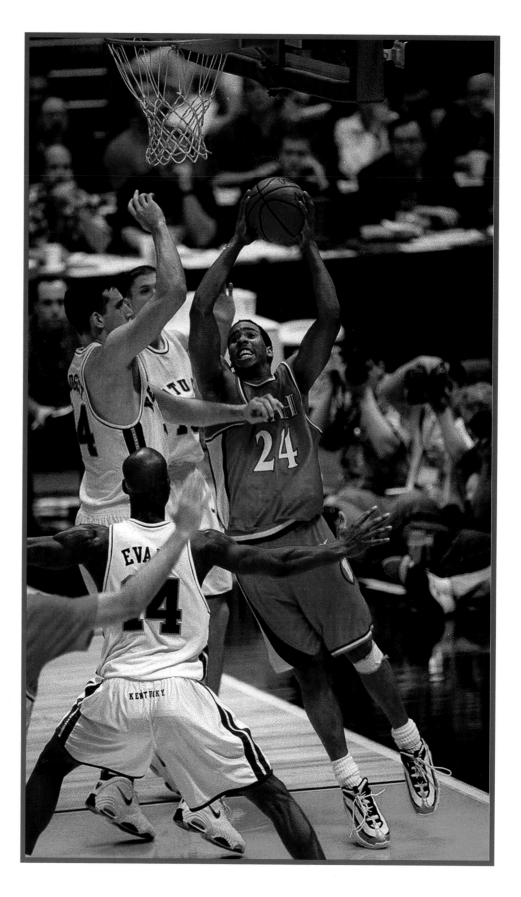

Utah's Andre Miller (24) could not muster his semifinal magic against Kentucky in the title game.

less than a national title would make his season a success.

Smith reached the Final Four with a team led by Scott Padgett, Nazr Mohammed, and Jeff Sheppard. Stanford, coached by Mike Montgomery, had a pair of talented guards in Arthur Lee and Kris Weems, and it played solid team basketball. Utah, under Rick Majerus, had two of the tournament's best all-around players in Andre Miller and Michael Doleac, while North Carolina returned under new coach Bill Guthridge.

Smith's troops were put to the test against Stanford, which got a superstar performance from Lee. The Cardinal took an early lead and held it right into the second half. Down 49-40, Kentucky crept back on clutch shots by Mohammed, Sheppard, and Allen Edwards. The Stanford players began to wilt under the Wildcats' renewed defensive pressure, and they found themselves down by 3 points with the final seconds ticking away. Again, it was Lee to the rescue. He canned a marvelous three-pointer to send the game into overtime. Smith kept his disappointed players focused, and they scored the first 5 points of the period. From there they gutted it out, 86-85.

Kentucky's opponent in the championship game was Utah, which defeated North Carolina in an exciting contest. In the first half, Miller was all over the court and Doleac confounded the Tar Heels down low as the Utes fashioned a 13-point lead. But Vince Carter and company chipped away and narrowed the score to 57-55 with a couple of minutes left. With the season on the line, Miller took control and hit a driving shot to give the Utes some breathing room. He then sank six free throws, as Carolina was forced to foul in the closing moments. Utah advanced, 65-59.

The NCAA Final began for Kentucky as so many other games had that year. The Wildcats poked and prodded opponents, fell behind, then used their superior bench strength to come charging back. Against Utah, Smith watched his team struggle against Doleac and trail at halftime, 41-31. Scanning the stat sheet, the Kentucky coach noticed that all five of Majerus's starters had logged a lot of minutes in the first half. He also knew that Utah's reserves were not very good. Smith started the second half by rotating fresh players into the game every couple of minutes, hoping to wear Utah down. Midway through the period, the Utes began to drag, and Kentucky exploded for 9 unanswered points to grab the lead. The Wildcats poured it on. A three-pointer by Cameron Mills was followed by a tough shot in the lane by Sheppard, and the game was as good as over. The final score was 78-69. Smith, considered by some to be an outsider, was now a genuine bluegrass legend.

> **Champion: Kentucky**
> **Winning Coach: Tubby Smith**
> **Number of Schools in Tournament: 64**
> **Best Player: Jeff Sheppard, Kentucky**

1999
Connecticut Huskies
Duke Blue Devils
Michigan State Spartans
Ohio State Buckeyes

Every few years, an unbeatable team reaches the Final Four, and all anyone can

ONLY THE BEST

Who are the greatest players in Final Four history? In the late 1980s, the NCAA chose its All-Time Tournament Team. The "starting five" was comprised of Lew Alcindor, Larry Bird, Wilt Chamberlain, Magic Johnson, and Michael Jordan. All-Decade squads were picked, too. These stars were honored for their performances in tournament play, however, not specifically in the Final Four. Indeed, the makeup of an "All-Final Four" team might look a bit different.

For example, Lew Alcindor might not make the list, despite having led the UCLA Bruins to three titles in three appearances. And Wilt Chamberlain, as great as he was, might not crack the "top three" Final Four centers. A much stronger case could be made for Bill Walton, who was utterly dominant in his three Final Fours. "Big Red" had two of the greatest shooting games ever (vs. Louisville in 1972 and vs. Memphis in 1973) and in his team's only loss (to North Carolina State) he scored 29 points and had 18 rebounds. And what of Bill Russell's two championships with San Francisco during the 1950s? Has anyone ever matched his end-to-end domination in big games?

Who are the two best forwards in Final Four history? This is a real argument-starter. Candidates for this position include James Worthy, Danny Manning, Richard Washington, Bill Bradley, Keith Wilkes, Corliss Williamson, and Christian Laettner. One thing most fans would agree on is that Larry Bird does not make this list. He may have been thrilling to watch during the 1979 tournament, but his struggles in the Final against Michigan State are hard to ignore.

do is root for a spectacular upset. With a string of 32 consecutive victories, the 1998–99 Blue Devils seemed to be one of those teams. Duke had a marvelous inside player in Elton Brand, a deadly shooting guard in Trajan Langdon, a capable floor leader in William Avery, and a defensive genius in Shane Battier. Still, Mike Krzyzewski was not expecting an easy Final Four. The Blue Devils were up against three schools that matched up particularly well against them. Michigan State, coached by crafty Tom Izzo, had an explosive star in

guard Mateen Cleaves and a solid supporting cast led by forward Morris Peterson. Ohio State had a pair of crack guards in "Scoonie" Penn and Michael Redd. And Jim Calhoun's UConn Huskies—who had held the number-one ranking for 10 weeks during the season—had a silky-smooth scorer in Richard Hamilton, as well as two excellent all-around guards in Khalid El-Amin and Ricky Moore.

Try as he might, Coach Izzo could not come up with any bright ideas to stop Brand in the first half of his semifinal game

A better choice might be Jerry Lucas of Ohio State, who competed in a total of six Final Four contests. He rebounded in double figures in every game, and shot the lights out in all but one. That game—the 1962 Final versus Cincinnati—saw the Bearcats' Paul Hogue put on a defensive clinic. Though he functioned as a center in Ed Jucker's system, the 6-9 Hogue could cover agile jump-shooters as well as 7-footers. And he was the only man who ever contained Lucas in a big game, which is reason enough to make him the second forward on an All-Final Four team.

It is hard to argue against Michael Jordan being included on any list of all-time greats, but does his winning shot in 1982 compare with Gail Goodrich's incredible one-man show in 1965? The UCLA star scored 42 in that game against the nation's best defenders. In his other three Final Four games Goodrich, netted more than 70 points. For the shooting guard position on the All-Final Four roster, the edge has to go to Goodrich.

As for point guard, Magic Johnson would seem like a slam dunk choice. But when you look a little closer at Michigan State's big wins over Penn and Indiana State in 1979, the most striking thing about his performance was his scoring. Johnson was indeed magical, but he had only five assists in the NCAA Final. Rumeal Robinson, a point guard for the Spartans' cross-state rivals, the Michigan Wolverines, was every bit as good in his Final Four games, if not better. Robinson was a floor general of the highest order in 1989, with 12 assists in an 83-81 win over Illinois and 11 assists in the overtime championship game against Seton Hall. Also, it was Robinson who canned the final free throws to give Michigan an 80-79 victory.

against Duke. The Blue Devils fashioned a 32-20 lead at the half, and they continued to trample the Spartans in the second period, when high-flying freshman Corey Maggette came off the Duke bench and put on a show. Then, just as Krzyzewski had feared, Cleaves went into the zone, and before the Blue Devils knew what hit them Michigan State was within four points. Duke barely survived, 68-62.

UConn and Ohio State jousted for 20 minutes, then took what they learned about each other and put it to work in the second half. With El-Amin and Hamilton leading the charge, the Huskies drew first blood and extended their one-point halftime lead to 10 points with 11 minutes left. Then it was the Buckeyes' turn. Bottled up for most of the game, Penn and Redd finally sparked a good run, and Ohio State pulled to within 3. Responding with tight defense and clutch baskets, UConn held off the Buckeyes to win 64-58.

Despite its solid performance in the semifinals, UConn was a heavy underdog against Duke. Coach Calhoun used this to

Ricky Moore, who made the game's key defensive play, celebrates UConn's win over Duke.

motivate his players. He told them that nothing short of a flawless defensive effort would be required to turn back the Blue Devils. The Huskies came out snarling, as El-Amin and Moore flustered Avery and Langdon with their intense defensive pressure. Hamilton, meanwhile, was hitting from everywhere. These were the matchup problems that had worried Krzyzewski, who felt lucky to have a 2-point lead at the half. In the locker room, Calhoun knew what was coming—Duke would start feeding the ball inside to Brand and win the game on rebounds and foul shots—so he collapsed his defense around the Duke center. This left Langdon open, and he began drilling three-pointers. Hamilton and the two guards kept pouring in points for UConn, however, and the Huskies held a 75-74 lead with less than a minute remaining. Langdon set up for a long jumper, but this time he was whistled for traveling. El-Amin converted a pair of free throws at the other end, and once again Langdon set up for a three-pointer. This time the Duke guard lost the ball to Moore, who prevented the game-tying shot with a great defensive play. Connecticut had toppled the mighty Blue Devils, 77-74.

Champion: Connecticut
Winning Coach: Jim Calhoun
Number of Schools in Tournament: 64
Best Player: Richard Hamilton, Connecticut

2000 AND BEYOND

2000
Florida Gators
Michigan State Spartans
North Carolina Tar Heels
Wisconsin Badgers

After Tom Izzo nearly beat Duke in the 1999 Final Four, few doubted that the Michigan State coach would return to challenge for a championship in 2000. By the time he did, Mateen Cleaves was playing like a miniature version of another Spartan great, Magic Johnson. Cleaves took control of games like no other player in the country, and Coach Izzo was happy to let him do so. Forward Morris Peterson also took a big step forward. The spectacular but erratic sophomore of 1999 was now a cool, confident junior. Expected to give the Spartans a run for their money was either North Carolina or Florida. The Tar Heels were led by do-it-all point guard Ed Cota, while the Gators played a fast-paced game designed by coach Billy Donovan, who had learned this approach as a player for Rick Pitino in Providence. Mike Miller and Teddy Dupay gave Florida two top-notch scorers—something that Donovan's mentor had not always had when he worked the sidelines for the Fri-

ars. The Wisconsin Badgers, under Dick Bennett, muscled their way into the Final Four on defense and rebounding. They were a dangerous team that refused to back down.

This was certainly the case in Wisconsin's semifinal against Michigan State. The Big Ten rivals knew each other well, and it did not take long for the game to turn into a street brawl. Elbows, knees, and shoulders were banging all over the court, as the teams put as much effort into intimidation as making shots. The two combatants staggered into the locker room at halftime with Michigan State ahead 19-17. Coach Bennett turned to his three-point shooters in the second half, but Jon Bryant and Duany Duany never found the range. Meanwhile, Peterson began to heat up for the Spartans. He hit three-pointers, layups, and everything in between. Michigan State pulled away for a well-earned 54-41 triumph.

In the other semifinal, Coach Donovan kept relentless pressure on Cota all game long, and the Tar Heels never got comfortable on offense. Miller and Dupay, on the other hand, settled right in and started scoring early in the first half. Carolina remained within striking distance until Cota got into foul trouble. The Gators surged to an easy victory, 71-59.

The experts seemed to have this NCAA Final all figured out. Slow-moving Michigan State would get run off the court by the fast-breaking Gators, and that would be that. What the experts did not know was that Coach Izzo's three floor leaders—Cleaves, Peterson, and Charlie Bell—had grown up together playing this up-tempo brand of ball in the playgrounds of Flint, Michigan. If Florida wanted to run, no problem—Cleaves and his running buddies would just play a little "summer ball."

In the opening minutes, the Gators caught Michigan State napping and got some quick points from big man Udonis Haslem. Cleaves pressed the action at the other end, where he broke off his drives and started nailing pull-up jumpers. Florida tightened its defense, but the Spartans made shots when they had to. The lead at halftime belonged to Michigan State, 43-32. Early in the second half, Cleaves attempted to drive around Dupay. He let out a scream as he rolled his right ankle and crumpled to the floor. Moments later, he was helped into the locker room, apparently done for the day.

Donovan implored his players to take advantage of this opportunity—Cleaves, he assured them, was a warrior. He would return. Cleaves's replacement, Mike Chappell, scored five points to keep Michigan State out in front. The Spartans' spirits soared a few minutes later when their point guard came limping out of the locker room. Playing despite searing pain, Cleaves inspired the team to an 89-76 victory. After the game, he got a big hug from none other than Magic Johnson.

Mateen Cleaves lets the world know who's number one. He bounced back from an ankle injury to turn in an MVP performance.

Champion: Michigan State
Winning Coach: Tom Izzo
Number of Schools in Tournament: 64
Best Player: Mateen Cleaves,
            Michigan State

SOME MAKE IT, SOME DON'T

Just how big a deal is it to reach the Final Four? Ask those who have been there, and they will tell you it is far more than just a career highlight—it is one of the highlights of their lives. For those who never made it, the Final Four is like a missing puzzle piece, because no matter how good you are as a basketball player, you can't get to the Big Dance unless you are part of a good team.

To really appreciate how special it is to compete in a Final Four, consider all the great college stars that never made it. You could put together quite a team picking just from those players. The list would include current NBA superstars Shaquille O'Neal, Tim Duncan, Jason Kidd, Paul Pierce, Karl Malone, Steve Francis, and Allen Iverson. And of course, players who jump from high school directly to the pros, like Kevin Garnett and Kobe Bryant, know they will never even have a chance to sample the excitement of college ball's greatest spectacle.

The list of all-time greats who never participated in the Final Four is long and impressive. You could build an entire wing at the Basketball Hall of Fame for them. It would include names like Paul Arizin, Charles Barkley, Dave Bing, Dave Cowens, George Gervin, Tom Heinsohn, Dan Issel, and Wes Unseld. At least these guys were lucky enough to play in the NCAA Tournament. Some of the biggest names in basketball never even got to the tourney at all, including Rick Barry, Billy Cunningham, Bob Davies, Julius Erving, Walt Frazier, Bailey Howell, Pete Maravich, Earl Monroe, Willis Reed, Bill Sharman, and Lenny Wilkens.

Alas, no matter how famous these players became, they never knew the thrill experienced by the likes of Paul Hogue, Anderson Hunt, John Kotz, Keith Smart, and Richard Washington—all of whom were named Most Outstanding Player. Although these Final Four legends did not go on to enjoy stellar pro careers, each can boast that he was the toast of basketball for one incredible moment in time.

2001
Arizona Wildcats
Duke Blue Devils
Maryland Terrapins
Michigan State Spartans

Everyone in the 2001 Final Four was playing for a cause. The Michigan State Spartans, minus graduates Mateen Cleaves and Morris Peterson, wanted to prove that they still had a championship program. Maryland's Terrapins had never been to the Final Four and were sick and tired of hearing they did not belong. The Duke players wanted a third national championship for Mike Krzyzewski, which would elevate him to all-time great status. And the Arizona Wildcats hoped to honor the memory of Lute Olson's wife, Bobbi, who had lost her battle with cancer during the season. The key players in this drama were Michigan State coach Tom Izzo, Maryland's wonderful inside scorers, Duke All-American Shane Battier, and Arizona's amazing collection of young talent.

The Duke-Maryland semifinal marked the fourth meeting between the teams during 2000–2001. Each game had been a war, and this one was no exception. The opening salvos were fired by the Terrapins, who bombed the bewildered Dukies to take an early 39-17 lead. No team had ever made up that large a deficit in Final Four play, but in the locker room at halftime Battier insisted it could be done. Playing a marvelous second half, sophomore point guard Jason Williams dared the Terrapins to come get him. This left the middle open for center Carlos Boozer, who was just getting his timing back after a midseason injury. Boozer teamed with Battier to neutralize Lonny Baxter, Juan Dixon, and Terence Morris, and the Blue Devils made it all the way back. With less than 10 minutes left, Duke barreled into the lead and mopped up the court with the dispirited Maryland players. The final score was 95-84.

In the other semifinal, neither team started well, and the game was up for grabs when the second half began. Then the Wildcats' offense started clicking, and they outscored the Spartans 21-3. Gilbert Arenas, Jason Gardner, and Richard Jefferson did most of the damage in an 80-61 win.

Two evenly matched teams faced off in the 2001 NCAA Final. For Duke to win, the Blue Devils had to contain 7-foot center Loren Woods and keep Jefferson and the other quick, powerful Wildcats under control. For Arizona to win, the Wildcats had to prevent Williams from penetrating and make sure Battier had only a good game

and not a great one. In the first half, Arizona gained the upper hand. Woods was killing the Blue Devils with clutch shots and powerful rebounds, while Williams picked up three fouls and had to go to the bench. The

Player of the Year Shane Battier hoists Duke's championship trophy after defeating Arizona in the NCAA Final. It was the third championship for the Blue Devils under coach Mike Krzyzewski.

Blue Devils did manage to shut down the other Wildcats—most importantly the backcourt twosome of Gardner and Arenas. After Williams picked up his fourth foul early in the second half, Coach Krzyzewski needed someone to step up and take charge.

That someone was Mike Dunleavy, perhaps the least-imposing player on the floor. The spindly sophomore had been shooting horribly, so at first Arizona was happy to let him fire away. Three 3-pointers later, the Wildcats were reeling. Instead of grabbing the lead with Williams out, they were suddenly down by 13 points. Arizona's big men—Woods and Michael Wright—started a comeback run, but there was Dunleavy again, with a pair of clutch baskets to keep the Blue Devils ahead. Krzyzewski then reinserted Williams, who finally began playing like a champion. He took over in the last few minutes and made big plays to keep the Wildcats at bay. The final score was 82-72. Coach K joined Bobby Knight, Adolph Rupp, and John Wooden as the only coaches to win three or more NCAA championships.

> **Champion: Duke**
> **Winning Coach: Mike Krzyzewski**
> **Number of Schools in Tournament: 64**
> **Best Player: Shane Battier, Duke**

2002
Indiana Hoosiers
Kansas Jayhawks
Maryland Terrapins
Oklahoma Sooners

The 2002 Maryland Terrapins did not fit the profile of a typical Final Four team. They had no McDonald's High School All-Americans on their roster, and the starting lineup featured only one or two players who looked good enough to make it in the NBA. What the Terps did have was experienced team leadership and an excellent work ethic. Coach Gary Williams relied on seniors Juan Dixon and Lonny Baxter to set the tone, and convinced his other players to follow their lead. Like Maryland, Indiana also lacked the over-the-top talent of past Final Four participants, but the players loved their coach and would do anything for him. Mike Davis earned their respect after replacing the legendary Bobby Knight, and he had the Hoosiers playing great defense and raining down shots from the perimeter. Kansas relied on the inside power of Drew Gooden and Nick Collison— a pair of 6-10 forwards who hoped to bring Roy Williams his first national championship since the 1980s—while Oklahoma was riding a wave of emotion following the courtside death of coach Kelvin Sampson's father a week earlier.

To reach the final, the Sooners had to get past Indiana. The Hoosiers got a solid game from forward Jared Jeffries, and gutsy performance from guard Tom Coverdale, who was playing on a badly sprained ankle, but still trailed 34-27 at the half. The difference was Oklahoma's inside play. During the intermission Davis told his players to get tougher in the paint. They came out on fire, hitting three-pointers and stretching the Oklahoma defense. That left room for reserve Jeff Newton to score a career-high 19 points from in close. The score was tied 60-60 late in the game, but poor shooting by Sooner guard Hollis Price and clutch free throws by the Hoosiers resulted in an 73-64 Indiana victory.

Maryland guard Juan Dixon (3) shoots in the NCAA championship game in the Georgia Dome, April 1, 2002, during first half play. Looking on are Dixon's teammate Drew Nicholas (12) and Indiana guard Dane Fife (11)

The other semifinal, between Maryland and Kansas, was viewed as the "real" championship, for both schools had been ranked #1 during the season and the winner would be heavily favored over Indiana. The Jayhawks opened up an early lead thanks to the three-point shooting of guard Jeff Boschee. But Dixon kept the Terrapins close. When Baxter was forced to sit with foul trouble, the wiry guard put the team on his back and gave Maryland the lead. With Baxter on the bench, sophomore Chris Wilcox and subs Tahj Holden and Ryan Randle did a great job down low, and the Terps had a seven-point lead after 20 minutes. The Jayhawks battled back in the second half, but Maryland pulled away with an 18-5 run. Dixon hit clutch baskets down the stretch for a 97-88 victory, which put the Terps in the NCAA Final for the first time in history.

For the Hoosiers to become the first number-five seed to win the tournament, they would have to shoot the lights out. Gary Williams knew this, and instructed his players to play tight defense all the way past the three-point line. Neither team shot well in the opening minutes of the championship game, which featured sloppy play and multiple turnovers. The only guy on the court who looked comfortable was Dixon, and he produced a marvelous first half. The Terps clogged the middle on defense, limiting Jeffries' effectiveness however, Coverdale picked up the slack and kept Indiana close. The Hoosiers trailed by 6 at intermission.

Indiana came out strong to start the final period, and grabbed a 44-42 lead. Dixon answered this run with a long three-pointer and a beautiful fadeaway jumper. Maryland's defense clamped down, and in no time the Terps had a double-digit lead. But Indiana battled back again, and cut the deficit to 4 points with just under 4 minutes remaining. Two great plays by Maryland senior Byron Mouton provided some breathing room, and the Terps went on to win 64-52.

Champion: Maryland
Winning Coach: Gary Williams
Number of Schools in Tournament: 64
Best Player: Juan Dixon, Maryland

For More Information

Some Good Books on the Final Four

Bjarkman, Peter. *The Biographical History of Basketball*. Chicago, Illinois: Masters Press, 2000.

Hirshberg, Al. *Basketball's Greatest Teams*. New York: G.P. Putnam's Sons, 1965.

Isaacs, Neil. *All the Moves: A History of College Basketball*. Philadelphia, Pennsylvania: J.B. Lippincott Company, 1975.

Johnson, Gary. *Men's Basketball's Finest*. Overland Park, Kansas: National Collegiate Athletic Association, 1998.

McCallum, John. *College Basketball, U.S.A*. Briarcliff Manor, New York: Stein & Day, 1978.

Packer, Billy. *50 Years of Final Four*. Dallas, Texas: Taylor Publishing, 1987.

Rice, Russell. *Adolph Rupp: Kentucky's Basketball Baron*. Champaign, Illinois: Sagamaore Publishing, 1994.

Rosen, Charles. *Scandals of '51*. New York: Holt, Rinehart and Winston, 1978.

Tarango, Martin. *Basketball Biographies*. Jefferson, North Carolina: McFarland & Company, 1991.

Index

Page numbers in *italics* indicate illustrations.

About the Author

Mark Stewart ranks among the busiest sportswriters today. He has produced hundreds of profiles on athletes past and present and has authored more than 80 books, including all 10 titles in **The Watts History of Sports.** A graduate of Duke University, Stewart is currently president of Team Stewart, Inc., a sports information and resource company in New Jersey.